SLOW BURN ENTREPRENEUR

SLOW BURN ENTREPRENEUR

Succeed on Your Own Terms
with the RELAX Method

MICHAEL WEBER

HOUNDSTOOTH
PRESS

SLOW BURN ENTREPRENEUR

Succeed on Your Own Terms with the RELAX Method

FIRST EDITION

ISBN   978-1-5445-4675-9 *Hardcover*
        978-1-5445-4674-2 *Paperback*
        978-1-5445-4676-6 *Ebook*

To my mom and dad, I know it wasn't easy raising me.

To my wife, Zeneyda, for understanding my ambition and giving me unwavering support. And to our kids, Nicol, Jacob, Jeremiah, and Christopher, because family is my reason why.

CONTENTS

"Success is not final, failure is not fatal:
it is the courage to continue that counts."

CONTROLLING CHAOS

"The life of an entrepreneur is total chaos!"

You hear words to that effect *all the time*. But I have a very different take: which is that the life of an entrepreneur is actually an escape from the chaos. An antidote to uncertainty. That's because, as business owners, we are in control of our own fates, as the following story will demonstrate.

Let me set the scene. I have been dabbling as an author since all the way back in 2013, which was when I first started drafting this book, a few pages at a time. My writing had largely fallen by the wayside when March 2020 brought with it the beginning of the COVID-19 pandemic, and I decided to return to my unfinished draft. At the time, the world was in turmoil, and we didn't know what was going to happen, how dangerous this new disease was, or how many lives would be lost.

My wife and kids were visiting family in her home country of Nicaragua when news of the disease broke in the US. During my business's Q2 quarterly meeting in early April, I impulsively decided to announce to the leadership team that I would be going to Nicaragua to be with my family. I booked a seat on a flight taking off one week later, which turned out to be the last flight into Managua, the capital and largest city in Nicaragua, before the entire airport shut down for an undefined period of time. I thought, *If this is the end, God help us, I'm going to spend all the time I have left with my wife and kids.*

I had to fly from Los Angeles to New York and through Mexico City with an overnight layover. The airports were ghost towns. It was apocalyptic. Like those zombie movies where one of the few survivors wakes up all alone and tries to find other humans. That was me in NYC's JFK airport in April 2020. Everything, I mean literally every business in the airport, was shut down except for one little sandwich shop, where the seven brave souls remaining in the entire airport flocked to find food. I wondered, *How are we going to make it through this?*

The plan was to spend one month in Nicaragua, living at the beach with my wife and some of her extended family away from civilization. But one month turned into two then two into three as the airports remained shuttered.

We made the best of our time in "lockdown."

My second youngest—he was two at the time—enjoyed romping with me on the white-sand beach of Playa Gavilan and in the tide pools of Punta Teonoste almost every morning. The whole family watched the vivid pink and orange technicolor sunsets together on the beach most nights. My wife's mother and sisters fed us some of the best Central American fare in the world throughout the day every day. Local fishermen's wives would come to our door to sell us the fresh catch of the day in the afternoons, sometimes mahi mahi or red snapper, sometimes lobster or octopus.

I was able to go surfing three to four times a week, usually at sunset, with my family waiting for me on the beach with a bonfire and a cold local beer. In the late mornings, I would lock myself in the master bedroom—my office—and write for a couple hours, then work remotely for a couple more hours, making sure "the trains were running on time" in my and my partner's business.

That business, which provided solar-panel and roofing products and services, was deemed essential by the great state of California, so we were never shut down completely, a blessing in itself. But the sales department, the management of which was my main leadership role in the organization, was not operating. (It was illegal to prospect for new customers during the first months of the COVID-19 pandemic response.) So, I was mostly excused from the day-to-day business activities—my business partner and our managers held down the fort while I was gone.

I remember thinking how lucky I was, as an entrepreneur, to be in a position to not have to worry, at least financially, for a while—and how fortunate I was to be enjoying the beaches in Central America with my wife and kids around me while most people were confined to their homes, struggling and stressed-out, wondering how they would survive this pandemic.

I knew far too many people whose livelihoods were in jeopardy because everything was shut down, including their workplaces. Psychologically, it was torture for many, and two people very close to me actually attempted to take their own lives. Some of you reading this, I'm sure, were in a state of constant anxiety, not knowing what the future would bring. Not knowing if your work would support you or if the government was going to step in and help.

But again, as business owners and entrepreneurs, to a large extent, we are in control of our own fates, which—for me, at least—made the whole situation easier to swallow and less nerve-racking.

THE SLOW BURN ENTREPRENEUR

I had two mentors over the last fifteen years who helped me grow into the business leader I am today. Both were men I worked for early in my career, and I respected them both a great deal.

One mentor appeared successful on the surface. He owned a big house, he always had the newest model truck and a nice speed boat, and his office spaces were large and luxurious. He was in constant motion, incessantly busy, with nonstop phone calls and endless meetings. He was focused on speed, on getting rich, on chasing that big payday. His need for speed and his propensity to burn through cash led to greed, fear, and a lack of trust among his employees. The pressure he put on himself and his staff to produce and grow was unsustainable, and he inevitably drove everyone away. In a fit of despondency, he died of a drug overdose, leaving behind millions in debt.

My other mentor, when I worked for him, did not appear successful. He rented his home, drove an old truck, and ran his business out of his garage. His office was a card table wedged in a corner that he would pull out for meetings. He spent time with his employees, listened to them, built relationships with them, and empowered them. His company felt like a family, and he treated his employees like members of his family.

Twelve years later, he owns the same company, the largest pest-control business in the state of Hawaii, and runs it with virtually the same personnel. He owns a sprawling, multimillion-dollar property with panoramic Pacific Ocean views on the east side of Oahu. He takes off several months every year to travel, trusting and allowing his people to run the business. His network is extensive, his investments will provide generational wealth to his kids, and he's not yet fifty years old.

He is a Slow Burn Entrepreneur. He thinks long term. He

thinks stability. He constantly invests in self-improvement and focuses on conservative, sustainable growth.

Which brings me to the overarching message of this book: owning your own business does not have to be that hard! Not only do I reject the idea that the life of an entrepreneur is total chaos, but my own entrepreneurial journey has also led me to reject the idea that you have to be your own slave-driver, running yourself into the ground in a never-ending grind.

You can breathe easy, knowing that if you foster the life-changing mentality it takes to be your own boss, you needn't worry about your results. They will come. This is part of why I titled the book *Slow Burn Entrepreneur*. Contrary to conventional wisdom, there's nothing wrong with growing slowly. You don't have to burn the candle at both ends in order to succeed, and your making it as an entrepreneur does not depend on your business becoming a juggernaut overnight.

Instead, you can **succeed on your own terms**. Isn't that the whole point of being an entrepreneur in the first place?

Let yourself *relax* and trust the process (the inputs), knowing that the income and profits (the outputs) are inevitable.

Let's break down the key word "relax."

R—Recognize your value. Becoming an entrepreneur means reprogramming your mind to understand you deserve more, and I'll show you exactly how to do that in this book. You'll start to see that most people are negative and cynical and that the inputs your psyche has received up until this point have probably not been the greatest for your success. You'll also be challenged to create your own plan for getting more of what you deserve by working on higher-value tasks more of the time and focusing on your prerogatives instead of taking orders from someone else.

E—Exercise Your Creativity. As an entrepreneur, you're

the one out front, making decisions and creating value. In this book, I'll show you how to develop the habits of generating your own ideas, reflecting on them, and choosing which ones to apply to your life and business. You'll start to see that, as a person with ideas who can effectively direct people, you're very much in demand. The masses crave direction, and the ability to think creatively will place you among the leaders of any industry.

L—Leap out of your comfort zone. Staying in your comfort zone, accepting your place in the muddy middle of life, is a surefire way to achieve if not mediocrity, at least a kind of stultifying normalcy. Yes, this is one way to go, but it's not your way. Armed with the insights from this book, you'll be able to start marching to the beat of your own drum and challenging the status quo. You'll learn to break rules and take extreme action to simplify your journey to success.

A—Act as if. This book also holds the secrets to time travel, in a sense. I'll show you how to act *as if* you are already the person you want to be in ten years. What sort of habits would that person practice in their daily routines? What kind of attitude would that person carry throughout their days? Learning how to act *as if* doesn't happen overnight, but I'll teach you the life hacks and habits that have worked best for me.

X—Examine your motivations. Finally, to "relax" as an entrepreneur you must diagnose your motivations and assess your goals to determine what it is you're actually working toward. Where are you going with all this? And if you are still in the daily grind of working for someone else, what sort of lifestyle are you putting off (until retirement) that you could be enjoying *right now* if only you had the time and freedom that comes with being your own boss?

I'll say it again: you can RELAX.

Think of the advice ahead as your permission to breathe. I

want you to feel how I felt when I broke free to succeed on my own terms. The following chapters will teach you the thought processes and habits I implemented—as a business owner and entrepreneur—to pull myself out of years of self-sabotage, unchain myself from the tyranny of a day job, and thrive. In particular, this book will teach you the methods and formulas I used to do the following:

- Build my business up to more than $10 million in gross annual sales.
- Work at my primary business no more than nine months per year.
- Leverage the power of what I call "extreme actions" to create extraordinary results for my business and get things done more smoothly.
- Leverage reflection and rest to ignite my and my business's creativity.

I am confident that once you see how a few simple practices can set you up for a lifetime of freedom and success, you'll be inspired to dive headfirst into the challenge of running your own business. I would love for you to experience the freedom and lifestyle that can come with being your own boss, and I hope this book is the impetus to you starting your own entrepreneurial adventure. I wrote it both as an empowering call for you to break out of the rat race and a practical guide to help you learn sales, entrepreneurship, and the incredible hacks I've picked up over the past fifteen years of my own journey. If you're already in the exciting game of entrepreneurship, I hope you can learn some new strategies and methods to make the game less risky and more fun. But if you're still stuck in a job that is "just a job," whether it's something you simply tolerate or actively despise, that's cool too: this book may be just the catalyst you need to make the leap you've long dreamed of but always put off.

Admittedly, this book started out as more of a self-oriented project. I only meant for it to be read by people within my own business and perhaps my kids when they're old enough to be curious about these ideas. But as it took shape, I started to see it as an opportunity to serve others by providing a roadmap for every person out there who is like the guy I used to be: someone who wants to start in sales and become an entrepreneur so they can free themselves from the drudgery of working for someone else.

And it feels like folks are hungrier than ever for this kind of advice. Since the world started to reopen amid the pandemic, I have been seeing more and more young people, in particular, who want to own their own businesses. They don't want to be dependent on a boss for a paycheck. To their credit, they have been paying attention to the ways the winds are blowing and know that when their job suddenly goes away, it can be a struggle to get back on their feet.

Several of my former salespeople have recently come to me out of the blue for advice on how to make the jump and launch their own businesses. It's weird. I feel like the answers they're looking for when they ask, "How do I start my own business?" are often treated like some ancient, mysterious formula. A black box of information that no one really knows how or wants to open. But that's all nonsense, and it doesn't have to be that way. This stuff *can* be taught and shared—and it can be easily learned and put into action! Beyond that, I believe when all is said and done the psychology and inner game of becoming an entrepreneur are just as important, if not more important, than the brass tacks of "how to."

If there is indeed a black box, I hope this book pries it open and helps bridge the gap between where you are now and where you want to be, giving hope and confidence to those willing to take the risk and break out on their own.

But I know that's all easy for me to *say*. Why should you believe it? Before we dive into the nuts and bolts, let me briefly address this understandable and important question: why should you trust me?

The truth is that for the fifteen years I've been in the game of sales and entrepreneurship (but especially in the early days), I've just been figuring it out myself through trial and error, one day at a time. I've experienced the ups and downs and adapted my habits to serve me and my business. I started as low as you can get on the totem pole, knocking on doors across the country for two years, before working my way up to running a home-security franchise, then opening my own solar-panel and roofing business nine years ago.

Ultimately, I developed and established practices that allowed me to level up my business to the point where it is now bringing in many millions of dollars each year. These practices also granted me the freedom to work only part of each year.

This is not a pipe dream. You can achieve the same. That said, though none of the strategies or tactics I detail in this book are particularly hard, they do require a dose of courage at the beginning—and some self-discipline to keep them going.

If you can learn these practices, make them your own, and properly implement them, there will be no stopping you on your road to success.

CHAPTER 1

YOUR PERSONAL HISTORY—IT MATTERS

"Nothing—absolutely nothing—in this life gives you more satisfaction than knowing you're on the road to success and achievement. And nothing stands as a bigger challenge than making the most of yourself."

—DAVID J. SCHWARTZ, *THE MAGIC OF THINKING BIG*

The beauty of being your own boss is there are no real hard-and-fast rules about starting a business. As funny as it sounds, you can kind of make it all up as you go. You have a blank canvas and the ability to paint whatever type and size of business you'd like.

You can base your business in your area of expertise or use what you learned from your college major. You can start a business to support your passion or capitalize on a hobby you're fond of.

You can try to shoot for the moon and build a $100 million company that will be taken public one day (even in this scenario, while it's not exactly a slow burn, you don't have to live a life of chaos). Or you can keep your operation small, opting to create a lifestyle business, one that doesn't cramp your vacation or family time.

It's up to you how big or small you want to go and how much time you want to invest. Some want a generational business they can pass on to their kids. Others want to build a company to eventually sell. And yes, some entrepreneurs want to build something quickly and sell it within five years. But for the most part, that's not who I wrote this book for.

No matter who you are or what your background is, your first step is understanding you can use your personal history to fuel your motivation. You can foster a positive outlook and belief that you can do it. I'll talk much more about this throughout this book, but the important point is you are capable of controlling everything that goes into your mind and training your brain to recognize and take advantage of opportunities as they come.

Take it from me: I'm nobody special, as you'll soon see. Here is a timeline of my professional life. It shows what kind of work I was doing, where I was in the world, and the level of success I achieved through that work. You'll notice it's been an up-and-down journey, to say the least. There have been plenty of failures—and while they weren't pleasant, that's alright because I kept at it, learning from those mistakes and finding greater success later on.

RESUME/TIMELINE

DATES	VENTURE	LOCATION	OUTCOME
2008-2009	Security Alarm Sales	MI, OH, PA, NJ, TX, MD, FL	Success
2010	Insurance Sales	MD, VA, DC	Success/Boring
2011-2012	Security Alarm Dealer	TX, CA, CO	Success
2012	Moved to Nicaragua to Learn Spanish & Surf	Granada & San Juan del Sur, Rivas, Nicaragua	Success
2013	Built a Movie Theater	San Juan del Sur, Rivas, Nicaragua	Failure, Didn't Make Money
2013-2014	Roofing Sales & Project Mgmt	CO, TX, IN	Success
2015-2016	Solar Dealer/ Franchise Owner	Rancho Mirage, CA	Success
2017	Built a Hotel on the Beach	Playa Gavilan, Tola, Nicaragua	Failure, Ran Out of Money
2017	Founded Solar Company	Naples, FL	Failure
Late 2017-2019	Solar Dealer/ Franchise Owner	San Bernardino, CA	Success
Early 2019	Founded a Roofing Company Insurance Restoration	San Bernardino, CA	Success
Mid 2019	Attempted Merger w/ a Company	CO, TX, CA	Failure
Late 2019	Roofing & Solar Company w/ New Business Partner	San Bernardino, CA and Denver, CO	Success
2025-2026	Build Casitas	Playa Gavilan, Tola, Nicaragua	TBD Pending Success

NOBODY SPECIAL

I grew up in a middle-class family in Fairfield, Ohio, a suburb of Cincinnati, with three younger brothers. My parents were high school sweethearts and both held degrees in engineering, but my mom chose to stay home with us and made sure we enjoyed the advantages of having a stay-at-home mom. She read to us from the time we were babies.

I didn't realize or appreciate it growing up, but we lived well. My dad worked as an engineer and earned an income in the top ten percent of the country. We had a nice house on a half-acre, and I had more opportunities than most of the kids growing up in my small town.

I was a runner and a swimmer, excelling at both in seventh and eighth grades. I elected to go to a Jesuit all-boys institution, St. Xavier, arguably the best high school for athletics and academics in the tri-state area of Ohio, Kentucky, and Indiana. They had won the state title in swimming ten years in a row, and I wanted to be part of their championship swim team. God bless my parents for paying the equivalent of a college tuition for me to pursue my high school dreams.

Despite my early swimming aspirations, I ended up excelling as a runner, becoming one of the best in the tri-state area my freshman year. That fall, I had my name announced over the school's PA system almost every week for winning races and setting records on cross-country courses across the city. It was a rush. Everyone knew my name, and even the football and basketball players showed me respect and gave me fist bumps and shout-outs in the hallways.

But I can't say I fit in at St. Xavier in every way. When I got there, it felt like my family suddenly became *lower* middle class because everyone else's parents appeared to be notice-ably wealthier than mine. One friend's dad was the orthopedic surgeon for the Cincinnati Bengals, and we often had bonfires and parties at his thirteen-thousand-square-foot mansion on his five-acre property in Indian Hill. I feel ashamed about it now, but I remember being resentful toward my dad at the time, repeatedly asking him, "Why didn't *you* become a doctor so we could be rich?" Back then, it seemed like such an easy, clear choice. Being a doctor meant being rich. So I devoted myself to the singular goal of getting into medical school.

I managed to take a whole year's worth of college classes while still in high school, mostly AP science classes, pushing toward my goal of getting rich as a doctor. At Ohio State University, I took two years of pre-medicine requisites, enough biology and organic chemistry to make my head spin.

The stress took its toll. I developed severe anxiety, mostly because I had gone from being a big fish in a small pond to a small fish in a big pond. I wasn't getting nearly the same attention or recognition as I had in high school, or even grade school. *Am I going to make it?* I would wonder. *All these kids seem smarter and more confident than me. And there's so many of them. How will I ever win?* I would go to class, try not to make eye contact with anyone, and get back to my dorm or apartment as quickly as possible.

Looking back, though I didn't know the term at the time, I had extreme agoraphobia: fear of social situations that caused embarrassment and panic attacks. I turned to alcohol, lots of alcohol, and marijuana to numb the pain and give me some semblance of confidence to attend social events and talk to my peers outside of class.

After a couple years of the pre-medicine track, I was burnt out on studying. The large quantities of beer and weed probably didn't help. I just wanted to graduate and get out of there as fast as possible, so I switched my major to marketing. I started getting into some higher-level business classes and was on track to be done with my marketing degree in three years.

In a class called Communications 505, or something of the sort, a young, enthusiastic teacher started the semester by having everyone stand up to introduce themselves and tell the class what they wanted to be when they grew up. I think literally all twenty-nine of my classmates wanted to have some high-powered position, like CEO, president of a Fortune 500 company, or Wall Street executive.

As for me, I introduced myself and let everyone know I wanted to be a "surf instructor in Hawaii." I had never even been to Hawaii, and I didn't know how to surf. But I was convinced money and power were not the solutions to happiness and I would be happiest with the *freedom* of living by the beach and teaching people how to surf.

That summer, I sold everything I had in the investment account I'd held since I was seventeen—about $4,000 (big bucks)—went out to Hawaii, and got my PADI SCUBA divemaster license in Kailua, on the east shore of Oahu. I reluctantly returned to Ohio State at the beginning of the fall semester, and after a two-year stint studying business marketing, decided to move out to Hawaii again to "finish my degree" at the University of Hawaii—Manoa. There, I endured another semester and a half before I figured it would be a better idea to drop out and move up to the North Shore of Oahu, the surfing capital of the world.

My parents, at that point, made the wise decision to cut their losses and cut me off financially.

For the first time in my life, I was on my own, and it was terrifying!

At the same time, I felt empowered to make my own decisions about my life. I had to sell my car to pay the rent, and I moved into an apartment behind a big mansion at Sunset Beach. We had no running water, no bathroom, and no cable. We did have a grill, on which we cooked *everything*, from pizza to the fresh fish we speared in the ocean, steps away. When I had to pee, I'd walk out the door and relieve myself in the field behind the small apartment, and when nature called, I'd ride my bike 250 yards down the road to the Sunset Beach public bathrooms.

It didn't take long for me to realize my glamorous job as a SCUBA teacher was not going to pay the bills. So, I took a full-time job as a "lunch lady" at a preschool in Kaneohe. Picture Chris Farley and Adam Sandler's "Lunchlady Land" from *Saturday Night Live* (worth a google if you don't know what I'm talking about). This required me to catch a bus at 5:00 a.m., before the sun came up, to get to the school at 7:00 a.m., two hours later. The bus ride home was even longer, three hours, so I'd get back up to the North Shore around 6:30 or 7:00 p.m., when it was dark again.

On the weekends, when I didn't want to ride the bus or was sick of waiting for it to show up, I would stick out my thumb and hitchhike up and down the North Shore. I had long blonde hair at the time, and tourists would frequently stop and pick me up, hoping to score some weed. Lucky for them, I usually had some! They would usually try to offer me money, and, not wanting to be a drug dealer, I would politely refuse and take a free ride to wherever I needed to go in exchange for a donation of some marijuana.

I was "living the dream," so to speak, on the weekends, teaching SCUBA diving and surfing, but I felt like I was a slave to "the man" all week, serving up food to preschoolers and washing dishes. A few months went by like this, and I was able to get good enough at surfing to start teaching surfing with my friends. Eventually, I was officially hired as an employee at

Hans Hedemann Surf School at Turtle Bay on the North Shore of Oahu. It may not seem like much, but I had finally made it—accomplished my college dream!

A fun aside—the movie *Forgetting Sarah Marshall* was filmed at Turtle Bay while I was teaching there. I actually met Jason Segel and drank a beer with him, looking out at the surf where he had just filmed. That was a surreal moment, and I realized these celebs we put up on a pedestal are just regular people like us. Jason Segel, great guy! (Mila Kunis, not such a friendly gal in person. But I get it.)

The five hours a day on the bus weren't all bad. I got to do a lot of reading. I've always been an avid reader. From the time I was little, it's something I've enjoyed. At the time, I read a lot of fiction books, my favorite authors being James Patterson and John Grisham. Luckily enough, a bus driver I had made friends with, Terry Pruitt, saw that I loved to read and gave me a book to try out. It was Tom Hopkins' *How to Master the Art of Selling,* and it was as thick as the Bible with tiny, intimidating print, not nearly as enticing as my John Grisham books. But I gave it a shot and was blown away by what it said. Apparently, there was this thing called "sales," and, allegedly, I could make more money in sales in a single day than I was making in two weeks as a "lunch lady." Lines like these caught my attention:[1]

> No one limits your growth but you. If you want to earn more, learn more. That means you'll work harder for a while; that means you'll work longer for a while. But you'll be paid for your extra effort with enhanced earnings down the road.

---

1   Tom Hopkins, *How to Master the Art of Selling,* ed. Warren Jamison, 2nd ed. (New York: Warner Books, 1982), 2.

And:[2]

In our profession no one limits your income but you. There are no income ceilings.

Remarkably, until encountering this book, I had no idea sales could be a lucrative profession. It had always been presented to me by my parents in a negative light, as a second-rate line of work that nobody wanted to be involved in. Little did I know my grandpa on my mom's side was a career salesman, and my grandpa on my dad's side had been a salesman and entrepreneur half his working life.

Turns out bus driver Terry was actively trying to recruit me into a network marketing insurance company called Primerica. And *How to Master the Art of Selling* was the first in a series of books from Terry that got me thinking about sales and entrepreneurship as a viable career option.

Then, when I started spending my Monday nights and Saturday mornings attending Primerica meetings down in Honolulu, I really started getting interested. It was there I discovered the middle class was doing it all wrong. I learned that the average person has a $40,000 net worth at age fifty-five and most people don't own their houses outright. The majority of our country's middle class are in debt up to their eyeballs with everything from car loans to credit card debt.

Through the meetings, I also started being exposed to different kinds of people. It was as if I had entered a world where everyone was friendly, positive, and hopeful about the future. It was amazing! Like a breath of fresh air. The more I thought about it, the more I realized most of the people I had known

---

2   Hopkins, *How to Master*, 1.

up to that point in my life (including my family and even my "carefree" surf and SCUBA buddies) were the opposite: negative, pessimistic, and cynical about the future. Moreover, the new people I was meeting seemed to be making some serious money, at least based on their clothes, cars, and prestigious addresses in neighborhoods across Honolulu.

Although I never got my insurance license—somehow, I failed the Hawaii test not once but twice—something had changed in me. I now knew there was another way to live. Becoming a salesperson and entrepreneur made so much more sense than working at a regular job for a paycheck.

After all, as a "lunch lady" or a SCUBA or surf instructor, it didn't really matter how hard I worked or how much I improved: the best I could do was an extra $20 tip at the end of the day or an extra 50 cents an hour. But as a salesperson, I could earn thousands of dollars more per month just by working a little bit harder and closing a couple more deals.

One day, my best friend on the North Shore, Bobby, taught a surf lesson to a couple of guys named John and Dave. They invited Bobby and me to dinner that night at the most expensive restaurant in Turtle Bay to pitch us an opportunity involving selling security. I was excited because I thought we were being invited to sell securities, stocks, and bonds, like the guys in the *Wall Street* movies.

John and Dave were in their late twenties but carried themselves like they were forty, exuding confidence and maturity combined with a sense of humor. And they both had kids, which impressed me because it made it seem like they had their lives together in every way even though they were roughly my age. Meanwhile, I was still riding my bike down the beach to poop at the public bathrooms.

It's not an exaggeration to say I was kind of in awe of them, and when the dinner was over, I knew I needed to do whatever they were doing. I didn't really understand yet what it all meant, or what the work would entail, but I knew it was an opportunity. Even though I had been "living the dream" for almost a year at Sunset Beach, it was time to grow up and make some money.

I talked to my parents about the idea, as well as to my best friends. They all thought I was an idiot and told me it was probably a scam. "If it sounds too good to be true," they said, "It probably is."

But what if it wasn't?

About a month later, I had a one-way ticket from Hawaiian paradise to the beauty and fair weather of…Detroit, Michigan. I was to join thirty returned Mormon missionaries in selling alarm systems (security) door to door in the summer of 2008, the peak of the worst recession our country had ever seen. My selling career and my journey into entrepreneurship had begun!

At the time, my brain was not ready to handle the roller-coaster ride of emotions—the extreme highs and lows—that is the daily struggle of door-to-door sales. Walking through the streets of Detroit posed all sorts of odd challenges—avoiding illegally organized pit bull fights, watching people burn their own houses down to collect insurance money, and having guns pulled on me weekly.

Each time I had a low moment and wanted to quit, I transported myself back to the painful, five-hour daily bus rides and the feeling of being squished between two large Samoans during the more crowded commutes. I needed a constant reminder of why I was working and why I couldn't quit. *If I could only make enough money to buy a car again*, I told myself.

I ended up doubling down on reading and personal development and became the top salesperson in the office. In fact, I sold enough that first summer that I was invited to join the top salespeople in the company on their glamorous year-end cruise of the Mexican Riviera.

I started realizing the benefits of my new habits, slowly molding my thought patterns to create positive change—and I haven't looked back since. Years later, I was able to parlay my sales success into building my own company, and I'd like to teach you to do the same.

I've spent almost this entire chapter telling you the story of my breakthrough in Hawaii and beyond because I want you to understand that *you* have a story too. And it's important. Our past doesn't determine our future. Anyone can change at any time. In this amazing society we live in, you have the power to take control of your life and be whoever you want to be. Just like me, you can use your personal history to fuel your motivation. You just have to train your brain, as we'll see in the next chapter.

CHAPTER 1—ACTION STEPS

- Think about what sort of business you want to build. At a glance, what appeals to you most: building a company to go public, a lifestyle business, or a generational business?
- If you already have a business, are you putting too much pressure on yourself to grow quickly and sell?
- Have you experienced some failures along the way? List them out. What did you learn from each, and what did the failure teach you that has become crucial to your current success?
- How can your personal story help fuel your motivation? Everyone has a unique path, a different road they've traveled.

CHAPTER 2

BRAINWASH YOURSELF TO SUCCESS

"Great men are those who see that thought is stronger than any material force, that thoughts rule the world."

—RALPH WALDO EMERSON

The mental work of becoming a business owner is 90 percent of the battle. Simply put, most people do not believe in themselves enough to make the leap into starting their own business. "Slow Burn Entrepreneur" is one thing, but you can't even get past the starting line if you don't make that leap. Unfortunately, far too many of us tell ourselves we're too young, too old, not smart enough, not rich enough, not connected enough—the reasons go on and on. If you fall into any of these categories, I'm here to *help you convince yourself* you are good enough, you are ready.

The first step is to realize you are an intelligent, creative person capable of handling whatever business ownership throws at you. Remember, this is the R in RELAX: Recognize your value. And the way to get there is to "brainwash" yourself with positivity so you can act despite feeling fear.

If you sincerely believe staying in your current job is the best long-term solution to your problems, stop reading now.

If you're ready to challenge the status quo, overcome your fear, and take some risks, keep reading.

The second step to what I call "positive brainwashing" is programming your subconscious mind to understand that fear and negativity have a very small place in our modern world. Entrepreneurs who have an abundance mentality and gratitude for how much opportunity is available in our society are the ones winning at this game.

Robert Kiyosaki, author of *Rich Dad, Poor Dad*, believes:[3]

> It's fear that keeps most people working at a job. The fear of not paying their bills. The fear of being fired. The fear of not having enough money. The fear of starting over... Most people become a slave to money.

YOU HAVE TO CONVINCE YOURSELF FIRST

Positive brainwashing is the method by which you convince yourself you are already successful and deserve more success. Your subconscious brain listens to both your internal and external dialogues and does not filter anything out.

Your subconscious does not understand sarcasm or humor. It takes everything at face value.

So, if your pet name for yourself is "dummy" and all day you're telling yourself, "Hey, dummy, you forgot to submit that

---

3   Robert T. Kiyosaki, *Rich Dad Poor Dad: What the Rich Teach Their Kids about Money—That the Poor and Middle Class Do Not* (New York: Business Plus, 2010), 48.

report," or "Hey, dummy, you sure made yourself look like an idiot with that girl," your subconscious mind begins to think you really are unintelligent and will steer you and your life in a way that reinforces that belief. You will have less confidence, take less risks, and, in general, live a smaller, less significant life.

From the ages of eighteen to twenty-four, I had some very self-destructive thought patterns that led to me habitually making bad decisions. This created quite a bit of trouble in my life. I couldn't keep a girlfriend. I couldn't hold down a job for more than a few months. I even wound up in jail almost ten times for various acts of stupidity. My mind was dominated by thoughts like *I'm a loser, I'm never going to make it,* and *Why try anyway? This world is so big and I'm so small, what does it matter?* I was terribly self-critical in my internal dialogue. In turn, my actions subconsciously guided me to become more of a loser, which led me to more drinking, drugs, and destructive behaviors.

It wasn't until I started brainwashing myself with successful thinking that I was able to change my actions and my life.

In his book *What to Say When You Talk to Yourself,* Shad Helmstetter shows why it's so important to have a positive internal dialogue. He explains that most of what we do is habit, ingrained in us from years of programming, usually by our parents. And that "as much as 77 percent of everything we think is negative, counterproductive, and works against us."[4] I love my parents, but they are both engineers by trade, and I was brought up to be suspicious of success and successful people. It was more important to study hard, not to take risks, and get a good job.

I had to use extreme measures to change my mental attitudes.

------

4   Shad Helmstetter, *What to Say When You Talk to Yourself* (New York: Pocket Books, 1987), 21.

One of the major ways I have been able to positively brainwash myself is by using affirmations, which is a tactic I learned about in Helmstetter's book. I started using affirmations when I was twenty-four years old. Back then, I would hand write and read them to myself every morning. Now, my affirmations are longer, and I type them out and record them on digital recorders to listen to while I'm trail running (more on digital recorders in Chapter 4).

This subconscious programming, or positive brainwashing, has helped me radically change my thought processes. I record my affirmations with the *Rocky* theme song playing in the background to further create a pump-up effect while I'm running and listening.

This may seem like the cheesiest exercise in the world, but I promise it works. I've done this for fifteen years, and now, my subconscious brain serves me. It finds me opportunities to reinforce my belief that I am successful and will become more successful. I make the decisions and take the actions in my life that are congruent with my strongly held inner beliefs about my own effectiveness.

I would encourage anyone interested in successful living to create their own version of affirmations. It's an amazing way to remind yourself of how special you are and how valuable you are to the world. You can find mine in the appendix of this book, along with a template to create your own.

AVOID THE NEWS LIKE THE PLAGUE

Ninety-five percent of the population grow up in "negative" households. I did. Like me, many people had a good upbringing and got a good education, but instead of having a positive, optimistic outlook on the world, they have a pessimistic, cynical one. Meanwhile, 95 percent of the country is not financially free, meaning they rely on their family, their employer, or the government to support them. Do you think there could be a connection, or is this just a coincidence?

I notice this bias toward negativity more often than ever these days. When I work with people I consider my peer group—college-educated individuals from good families—I find almost all of them somehow have the opposite of rose-colored lenses when looking at their world.

And there's a very good reason for this pessimism.

I believe the twenty-four-hour news cycle is to blame. Most people, in particular those from educated families, like my engineer parents, think it is important to watch (or read, scroll, etc.) the news every day to "stay informed." I call bullshit. The only thing we are staying informed about is what celebrity died that day or what horrific weather event is going to wreak destruction on the country. Whatever news event is going to be the next big fear the media can sell us for weeks on end—that's the news.

The main goal of modern news seems to be to tell us what we should be fearful about today. Is there a major Ponzi scheme robbing millions from desperate people? Is there a war in the Middle East that is doomed to eventually come to US soil? Was there yet another school shooting, killing innocent kids? Are there too many immigrants crossing the border and taking our jobs? Is there a worldwide pandemic, and we should all stay in our houses? Bodies in the streets?

Fear drives ratings (and clicks), which generate money, making fear very profitable. For this reason, mainstream news focuses on the stories and opinions that will inspire the most and longest sustained fear in its audience. If you don't believe it has become this depressing (and I make my wife do this whenever she insists on watching the news), do a quick exercise. Just watch a thirty-minute segment of local or national news and jot down the subject headlines of each of the five to ten highlighted stories. For example: murder at a liquor store, police officer found guilty of manslaughter, body found, rape victim found alive in critical condition, charity giving away puppies for cancer, high-speed chase killed two, hurricane in the Gulf, rainy weather coming next week.

Now, determine the ratio of depressing and negative stories to positive and uplifting ones. Usually, it's about an eight-to-one or ten-to-one ratio of depressing and negative to positive and uplifting. Then, ask yourself, *Did it benefit me in any way to spend thirty minutes of my life watching the news? Is there anything I could personally do to have a positive effect on the things I saw? Or am I just reinforcing the beliefs I have about how terrible the state of the world is and why I shouldn't try because we're all screwed?*

Fear sells. The news networks know it. That's why you can't help but to slow down when passing a bad crash on the freeway. *How bad was it?* you wonder. *Was anybody killed?* It's why our eyes are glued to the TV when watching a high-speed chase. *When's he going to crash? I know he's going to crash any minute; it's going to be bloody.* It's called "disaster porn."

Facebook News Feed and Apple News make it even easier to spend all our time doom-scrolling and obsessing over what's wrong with the world. This has a very powerful effect on kids, making them think the world is a scary, evil place and someday soon it will come to an end.

The reality is we in the US live in the best civilization that has ever existed, with more technological advances than the world has ever seen. Everything is at our fingertips with the click of a button, and "Americans have more disposable income than nearly every other country on earth."[5] We live in a golden age that people have looked forward to for thousands of years. Think ahead: what will the history books write about this time five hundred years from now?

Are there problems? Yes, absolutely. The world has always had and will always have problems. But, in my view, the real problem in our modern lives, thanks to television and the internet, is that we know everything we need to fear *ALL THE TIME*. And we know what's coming. What we should worry about next week. There's a hurricane off the coast. There's a disease spreading in China. Mexican cartels have infiltrated the United States. There are terrorists from 9-11 still living in our country, planning their next attack. There's a global debt bubble that could burst at any moment.

I noticed at a recent sales-recruiting class we had at our business that this attitude of "Why try? The world is going to end soon" has become particularly popular among young people graduating into adulthood. I observed that younger Millennials and much of Generation Z have a mentality of "It's better to just hunker down and punch the clock at work, binge Netflix, play video games, and let the world pass by rather than actually try to make something happen in life."

Over the last three years, I've noticed a trend when recruiting new talent to our business. Many young people expect to live without any adversity. It's fascinating to watch them come in and assume they'll be handed a job, given money, and not have to work or struggle for it at all. Just show up and collect a paycheck with the greatest of ease. They harbor an entitlement

---

5   Ryan McMaken, "Why Do Americans Have Such High Incomes and So
     Little Savings?," *Mises Wire*, August 26, 2016, https://mises.org/mises-wire/
     why-do-americans-have-such-high-incomes-and-so-little-savings.

attitude of "the world should take care of me, and it should be a cozy place for me to exist in and pass my years."

A new attitude needs to be instilled in young people. They need to be woken up and reprogrammed. And the new attitude needs to be positive. Number one—we live in a country that has more personal liberty and opportunity than almost anywhere on Earth. If you don't believe me, do some quick interviews with El Salvadoreans or Guatemalans who have made it illegally into our country. They risked their lives walking across the desert for days on end and crossing a deadly river in the middle of the night, sometimes *multiple* times, to get into the land of the free. They are excited for the *opportunity* to wake up early and go to work every day at some of the most menial labor jobs our country has to offer.

(Granted, once the money has been made in the US, there are better places to spend it where the dollar goes much further. Hence, my investments and time spent in Central America. At current writing, 720,000 retirees from the United States are receiving their social security checks abroad. But I digress.)

To be successful, you need to understand your life will *not* be free of struggle. There will, no doubt, be times when you have stress and anxiety, times when things don't come easy. Welcome these small doses of suffering, and take them in stride. Embrace the challenges, and know they have the power to shape your character into a resilient, capable winner.

Number two—our standard of living, that we so take for granted, is mind-blowingly, ridiculously luxurious and easy compared to life just one hundred years ago. A century ago, it was still common to see a horse and buggy roll down a main road in a major city. Most homes did not have indoor plumbing. That meant you had to walk outside to use an outhouse as a restroom. And you sure didn't have a hot-water shower to warm you up on a cold day.

We no longer need to worry about finding adequate food, except for a trip to the grocery store once a week. We don't have barbarian invaders who might kill us and kidnap our families. Instead, we have hackers who might hack into our Amazon accounts. Instead of taking the Oregon Trail across the country for two years and losing half our family and friends to hunger and disease, we can take a first-class flight for $1,000 from New York to LA and arrive unscathed in five short hours.

With the internet, the barrier to entry for almost any opportunity is so low, it makes our options overwhelmingly endless.

You want to be a writer? Self-publish on Amazon or start responding to questions on Quora and get your name out there.

You want to be a doctor? Find a medical mission trip to a developing country or volunteer in a level 1 trauma center in the inner city where they give you privileges to do things fourth-year medical students don't.

You want to be a business owner? Buy things from your nearest port city off the ships from China and sell them on eBay or Amazon, out of your house, on the street corner, at a farmers market, or door to door.

You want to learn from the smartest people on the planet? The movers and the shakers? Go read their books. Most of them have written at least one already. You don't like to read? You want to hear them speak? Download their audiobooks on Audible, look up their TED Talks, find their YouTube videos, or join MasterClass or Headway and they *will talk to you from your phone.*

But for God's sake, stay off of CNN, stay off of Fox News, stay off of your Apple News feed. You will poison your brain with negativity and pessimism. Watching your friends' Facebook feeds will give you a bad case of FOMO, fear of missing out. *Why work so hard when my friend Johnny plays Call of Duty all day and look how cool his life is?*

Read books titled *The Magic of Thinking Big, The Laws of Success in Sixteen Lessons, 177 Mental Toughness Secrets of the World Class, Think and Grow Rich,* and *The Happiness Advantage,* just to name a few.

It's time to make your car a positive-brainwashing university. No more radio or music, unless you're on vacation.

Listen to the classic business thinkers, like Jim Rohn, Dale Carnegie, Napoleon Hill, and Wayne Dyer. Tune in to the modern gurus, like Tony Robbins and Peter Drucker. Get yourself programmed by the new experts: Tim Ferriss, Gary Vaynerchuk, and Grant Cardone. Subscribe to David Goggins and Jack Canfield or any positive psychology expert who will inspire and motivate you.

Use your time in the car for the daily mental tune-up you need to be the person you always knew you could become. Study positive books every morning for at least an hour. Read this book six more times.

Once you have your internal environment under control, it's time to relearn how to "put your thinking cap on." The good news is thinking and creating are two of the highest-paid skills you will ever learn. That's the topic of our next chapter. But before we move on to Chapter 3, let's look at a real-life example of a great slow-burn company. From here on out, in between chapters, you'll find a short profile of an exemplary slow burn company or alternately, a cautionary tale of a get-rich-quick company.

CHAPTER 2—ACTION STEPS

- Examine your self-talk objectively. Keep a log of how you are talking to yourself. Is it encouraging when you have a win and forgiving when you mess up? Do you have a habit of pumping yourself up or cutting yourself down?
- Decide now to catch yourself when you tell yourself something critical. Stop in the moment, write down the critical statement you just told yourself, and then write a contradictory, positive statement or an uplifting speech pattern you can adopt for next time.
- Take fifteen minutes and create your own affirmations using the template in the appendix. Start reading these to yourself every morning, or record them and play them back when you are exercising.
- Evaluate the inputs into your life and mind. What media are you consuming and for precisely how long each day? Keep a log on your phone or in a journal to keep track.
- Ask yourself, "How can I change my media consumption to tip the scales in my favor—toward positivity and away from pessimism, doom, and gloom?"

INTERLUDE—W. L. GORE & ASSOCIATES, *SLOW BURN* COMPANY

Wilbert L. Gore and Genevieve Gore, a husband-wife duo, founded W. L. Gore & Associates in 1958 in Newark, Delaware, with a $5,000 investment. The company's first invention was PTFE (polytetrafluoroethylene) tape, branded as "Plumber's Friend," used for sealing pipe threads.

In the late 1960s, Wilbert and Genevieve's son Bob was researching a method to stretch PTFE into pipe thread tape. One day, he stumbled upon a discovery while stretching a rod of PTFE resin, a material known for its extraordinary properties. Instead of breaking, the material expanded, forming a lightweight structure with millions of tiny, interconnected pores. This marked the birth of expanded PTFE (ePTFE), the foundation of Gore-Tex.

Bob Gore recognized the potential of ePTFE for various applications, including outdoor and hunting gear. However, rather than rushing the product to market for quick profit, W. L. Gore & Associates took a patient and meticulous approach to development.

Their commitment to being a "slow burn" company rather than trying to get rich quickly was evident. Gore-Tex, which would become one of their most iconic products, could have made them a fortune in a short period of time in the early 1970s.

Instead, for nearly seven years, the company invested in research, testing, and refining the technology. They worked to perfect the manufacturing process, ensuring the material met rigorous quality standards. It wasn't until 1976 that Gore-Tex, the revolutionary waterproof, breathable fabric, was introduced to the market.

This story illustrates W. L. Gore & Associates's emphasis on quality and a long-term outlook on business. The company's leaders were most interested in creating a game-changing product that would provide lasting value and maintain the company's reputation for excellence, even if it meant waiting years for a return on their investment.

The patient and deliberate approach to developing Gore-Tex paid off tremendously. The product revolutionized the outdoor-apparel industry and had extensive applications in numerous other fields, from medical devices to industrial uses.

The success of W. L. Gore & Associates showcases the advantage of their commitment to being a "slow burn" company, prioritizing quality and innovation over quick gains. It has been a defining feature of their business philosophy and long-term performance since the beginning and helped the company grow to twelve thousand employees and $4.5 billion in revenue in 2022.

CHAPTER 3

THE HIGHEST-PAID SKILL IN THE WORLD

"The single most powerful asset we all have is our mind. If it is trained well, it can create enormous wealth in what seems to be an instant."

—ROBERT KIYOSAKI

Kids are extremely creative from birth. They have to be. They are figuring out the world one touch, smell, and taste at a time. That's why my kids had a fascinating ritual of putting everything in their mouths, even the stale pieces of popcorn they found under the couch three days after movie night.

From the time we are kids, however, our creativity is squashed, as our parents repeatedly tell us "no." We're disciplined for exploring places we shouldn't and told everything we ought not do or cannot have, oftentimes in an embarrassing public chastising.

Worst of all is how we're scolded most harshly as kids when embarking on our most daring adventures. Kids will climb to the highest point in a room despite having no idea how to get down. They'll attempt to make the jump from one couch to another with no thought to a bloody lip or broken bone. These behaviors are human nature. Testing our boundaries and creatively challenging ourselves is the natural way of things.

However, school trains us to stand in lines, follow orders, and speak only when spoken to. We are taught to become followers, sheep in the herd.

I was a good, obedient sheep in grade school and high school, and most people are. My parents taught me well, I had great manners, and I studied and got good grades. I remember being very good at most things when I was told exactly *what* to do.

However, in creative endeavors, where I was given only abstract instructions and had to actually think on my own and come up with *what to do*, I was completely helpless. I would draw total blanks in these imaginative endeavors, especially in art class. If I was told to sketch a mountain with a river, I could muster through and squeak out a B+. But if the assignment was to "Draw whatever you feel like," or anything similarly vague, I was routinely paralyzed. Most of my classmates, minus the artists, were in the same boat.

Do as you're told and get it done right, inside the lines. This is the employee mentality embedded in our society, whether intentionally or not. There is very little creative problem-solving being taught. This is also the reason the masses crave direction: a job with a paycheck and a clear set of instructions telling them what to work on.

But this is also why there is such demand for the entrepreneur, the independent thinker. The man or woman on the white horse to whom everyone else looks for vision and direction.

I'll say it again: thinking and creating are the highest paid skills in the world.

Most entrepreneurs who have achieved massive success did so outside the box, outside a school or work setting, thinking autonomously.

Look at Sara Blakely, the founder of Spanx. She was constantly dreaming up ideas and honing her entrepreneurial skills in door-to-door sales and eventually came up with a solution to a billion-dollar problem. She came to the realization that men were historically the ones responsible for designing women's undergarments, all the way up until the 1990s. She proceeded to revolutionize the industry by using a woman's perspective.

Howard Schultz came up with the idea for the modern Starbucks cafes while on a trip to Italy. He wanted to replicate a place where people could come, congregate, and socialize while drinking quality coffee.

Early in my sales and entrepreneurial journey, I observed that always doing what I was told was not the formula to get ahead. Even worse, *waiting* until I was told to do something was one of the least effective approaches I could take. In fact, waiting to be told to act and then doing that action exactly the way everyone else does will almost always guarantee mediocrity and a life of insignificance.

The good news: creativity and outside-the-box thinking can be learned (or, rather, relearned since we were all creative geniuses as children!). So RELAX. And pay special attention here to both the E part of that equation, which is to "exercise your creativity," and the L, which stands for "leap out of your comfort zone."

NURTURE YOUR OWN CREATIVITY

To cut your own path in this world and rise above the millions of sheep who rely on a boss to tell them what to do, you must use intentional, disciplined creativity. Despite struggling in my early years, even I (someone completely flummoxed by a simple art assignment in grade school) have become a competent, somewhat-creative thinker using certain practices.

Okay, maybe it's generous to call it creativity. I would more accurately describe it as gathering ideas from other smart people who have come before me, constantly reflecting on daily life, and devising incremental improvements. Sir Isaac Newton famously stated, "If I have seen further, it is by standing on the shoulders of giants."[6]

Reading is the secret first step to gathering ideas. The average person in the United States reads 12.6 books per year and earns $77,178.[7] The average CEO reads more than three times that per year and earns $630,000 per year.[8] Leaders are readers, simply put. To quote a popular saying, "The man who does not read has no advantage over the man who cannot read." The reason the top 2 percent continue to be successful is they keep learning. They keep feeding their minds with useful knowledge and ideas.

Here's my method for nurturing creativity in my life. First, I read constantly about sales, business, happiness, and success. I try to make sure I get in an hour or two a day of reading on one of those subjects. All of these books give me food for thought throughout the day. It is amazing to think just how much quan-

---

6   Isaac Newton to Robert Hook, 5 February 1675, Simon Gratz Collection, 9792, Historical Society of Pennsylvania Digital Library, https://digitallibrary.hsp.org/index.php/Detail/objects/9792.

7   Jeffrey M. Jones, "Americans Reading Fewer Books Than in Past," Gallup News, January 10, 2022, https://news.gallup.com/poll/388541/americans-reading-fewer-books-past.aspx; Alexandra Olson, "CEOs Got Smaller Raises. It Would Still Take the Average Worker 2 Lifetimes to Make Their Annual Pay," PBS News Hour, May 31, 2023, https://www.pbs.org/newshour/economy/ceos-got-smaller-raises-it-would-still-take-the-average-worker-2-lifetimes-to-make-their-annual-pay.

8   SalaryCube Editorial Team, "What Is the Average CEO Salary by Company size?" SalaryCube, January 25, 2024, https://www.salarycube.com/compensation/what-is-the-average-ceo-salary-by-company-size/.

titative value can live inside one single book. Suppose someone who is fifty years old writes a book based on twenty years of experience in a particular subject, such as how to relate better to people. Now, let's say I read that book in five hours. I've just condensed twenty years of experience and trial and error on how to better relate to people into five hours. Granted, I'm not going to become a master communicator in that little time, but I'm definitely going to avoid some of the pitfalls and mistakes the author endured over the twenty years they spent researching the subject.

When sales are down, I read Brian Tracy or Grant Cardone and find some sales training I can use to motivate my guys. When my own motivation is lacking, I reread something by Jim Rohn, *The Magic of Thinking Big*, or anything by Napoleon Hill. When I'm stressed out and working long hours, I know I need some Wayne Dyer, and I'll go back and listen to one of his seminars. If our business is lacking ideas, I'll revisit some of the creative ideas in Tim Ferriss's books. If our business management feels inefficient, I'll take another look at a classic Peter Drucker book and his eternal management wisdom.

Within my peer group, we have a habit of diagnosing one another's problems with books. I'll cite a problem with a new star employee, and my friend Nick will say, "Have you read *Principles* by Ray Dalio? Take a look at Chapter 3." Or I'll mention an issue with a manager in our business, and my friend Dan will say, "That reminds me of a book by Richard Branson. He says you should never compromise on a decision like that." If ever a manager in my company tells me they're overwhelmed and have too much on their plate, too many balls in the air, I send them a photo of *The Effective Executive* by Peter Drucker and tell them to grab it or download the audio as soon as possible.

It's virtually guaranteed that you'll gain at least a few golden nuggets from each author. But the key is implementation. Even if it's one line or one tactic, start using that new skill immediately. Let's suppose you learn that the most effective way to use your eyes in a conversation is to maintain eye contact 72 percent of the time and use your eyeballs like tanning lights, moving up and down your prospect's face. Try that technique ten times in the next thirty days. If it works for you, if it's effective, add that arrow to your quiver of skills.

To further emphasize the importance of reading and shamelessly name drop, I met Hollywood sweetheart and *Barbie* superstar Margot Robbie in Los Angeles a few years ago in a speed-reading class. It was a couple years after her breakthrough performance in *The Big Short*, so she was honing her skills to be able to read more scripts faster. I was learning how to read more business books.

When I tell our salespeople they should try to buy one new book a week, they often complain about the price.[9] But that's a silly excuse when you think about it. Let's say you spend $20 on a book, and you get one idea, a golden nugget, that will make you an extra $50,000 over the next two years. Was that book worthwhile? Of course it was! Even if the idea only profits you an extra $1,000 dollars this year, it was worth fifty times your initial investment.

---

9 I no longer give away books. It's important that people buy them themselves. It may seem illogical, but I've found most people just don't value a free book enough to put in the time to read it.

FIGHT IGNORANCE—HIRE A COACH

"The most honest, 'self-made' man ever was the one we heard say: 'I got to the top the hard way—fighting my own laziness and ignorance every step of the way.'"

—JOHN C. MAXWELL

Admitting you must fight your own ignorance every step of the way requires a strong character and lots of humility. You need to make a conscious effort not to be the entrepreneur whose business hits $1 million and they think they've made it. Doing so will make you uncoachable and, often, complacent. This is the "R" in our RELAX acronym, recognize your value. Once you've leveled up to a seven-figure business owner, you may feel confident in making a living, but you still have a long way to go to build your company into something that can truly make a difference.

Unfortunately, it is very common that after their first taste of success, many business owners become overly confident. At that point, the average entrepreneur is no longer willing to look for ways to improve. They stop reading, stop creating new processes for their staff, and think they have "arrived." They effectively put a glass ceiling on themselves, their learning, and their earning capacity.

Don't let that be you. Set the bar high from the outset. Understand that even after your business does $5 million or $10 million in a year, you are still capable of doing better. Still capable of learning more.

The best investment you could ever make in yourself and your personal development is to hire a coach. Don't try to do it all on your own. Coaches are trailblazers who have gone before us and thoroughly enjoy coaching, usually in their retirement, after long, successful careers. Take advantage of the wisdom they've gained over a lifetime of trials and tribulations in business.

The first time I hired a coach was thirteen years ago, and he set my life on track by helping me figure out what I really wanted. It was a ninety-day program, and there was lots of homework involved in addition to weekly calls. At the time, it cost me my life savings, but it was worth every penny.

I've had the same coach now—his name is Marc—for six years. He's not cheap at $275 per hour. But the two hours I spend with him are some of the most valuable of my whole month. He helps guide me—in business and in life.

We had another excellent business coach, Brian, who worked with our company for a year. He conducted all of our quarterly meetings and our annual planning meeting. He also facilitated our management meetings, helped us make plans and decisions, and held us accountable.

Again, both of these men, Marc and Brian, have already run the gauntlet, so to speak. They have successfully achieved what I am in the midst of attempting. Brian built a multimillion-dollar engineering firm that sustains itself, and he now lives in the "owner's box," attending only the board meetings for his company and coaching full-time. Marc built and sold his company years ago and now coaches young entrepreneurs who wish to do the same.

To get the most out of my coaching calls with Marc, I spend the week leading up to them jotting down the biggest issues I'm facing in my life and business. I rank these in order of importance to make sure I discuss them with Marc. Then, on our biweekly call, he really helps me see my life and work from an outsider's perspective, looking down from the ten-thousand-foot level, instead of from "on top of the ant hill" of my life, where I stand every day.

A good coach is skillful at asking the tough, high-level questions for you to dig into and help you decide if this is what you

really want. Do you really want to take on a new business partner? Does this new partner have a value match? Does this new
project you're considering fit into your core focus as a business?
Is this taking you toward your ultimate goal, partially retiring
at forty and spending more time with your family? Have you
talked to your wife about it yet? How does she feel about it?
(This one always gets me thinking, *He's good!*)

Coaches are experts at learning your decision-making
strengths and weaknesses. Therefore, they are the best people
to ask the tough questions that help guide you.

As for Coach Brian, he keeps our business focused on
long-term goals by setting up a handful of ninety-day goals
and holding us accountable to hit them. He works within an
organization called EOS, the Entrepreneurial Operating System.
Brian is a sounding board, and through his twenty-some-odd
clients, he is able to compare our ideas and results with other
companies. If we're not hitting our goals, Brian makes sure we
set more reasonable targets for the next ninety days.

We set our "rocks," or goals, every quarter, ones that will
bring us closer to our one-year goals. The idea is that businesses
that try to push toward goals that are too far into the future will
either burn out or get distracted. They can also lose steam while
marching along in their normal course of business and struggle
to chase a goal five to ten years into the future.

Working in ninety-day increments serves the dual purposes
of mitigating distractions and improving focus and clarity. We're
forced to determine the best roles, or "seats," in the company
and make sure we are filling those seats with the right people.
We bring up "people issues" and score our employees based on
our internal company values. Then, we make hiring and firing
decisions based on those values.

Brian is essentially a fractional CEO, helping us run our

business for the equivalent of an admin's salary of $25,000 per year. It's amazing what we get done in our quarterly one-day sessions with him. Our leadership team walks away energized by the fact that we have a clear path to run on for the next ninety days.

In an effort to simplify the life of business owners, EOS advises businesses to only take ninety days at a time. EOS is centered around the principles taught by Gino Wickman in his book *Traction*. If you ever feel you are lacking rhythm in your business, or it feels like controlled chaos, I highly recommend *Traction* and EOS.

EOS's claim to fame is it is the business operating system behind the real estate empire RE/MAX. Seven thousand businesses across the country run on this system, and it is a well-known business operating system that is adaptable to any industry. As a bonus, if you go to sell your business one day, you are more attractive to a buyer with a business operating system in place.

Owens Corning, one of the two biggest roofing manufacturers in the nation, promotes the EOS system to all of its contractors via its website.

SUMMARY

The get-rich-quick business owner is ego-driven and thinks he has all the answers. He doesn't appreciate the wisdom available in books or seek advice from coaches. He's always focused on short-term profits, and he's too busy with his nose to the grindstone to invest in self-development.

The Slow Burn Entrepreneur, on the other hand, is humble and knows there's always more to learn. He devours books, presentations, and podcasts that will energize his mind and provoke his creativity. He's on an endless search for information that will provide seeds for innovative thought in his daily life as a business owner. He finds coaches to support his decision-making and solicits advice from anyone further along on their path to success. The Slow Burn Entrepreneur realizes that investing in himself through personal development is the best investment he could ever make. He knows that by trusting in the process, seeking out quality inputs for his mind, he's able to succeed on his own terms, time and time again.

Now that you've learned a little more about the highest-paid skills in the world, let's look at another way to spark creativity and gain the upper hand on your competition: Idea Mining. That's the topic of our next chapter.

CHAPTER 3—ACTION STEPS

- Ask yourself: do I consider myself a creative person? If not, think about why you see yourself that way.
- Brainstorm ways you can actively practice your creativity.
- Identify books you can read this year to help generate ideas to apply to your life or business.
- Devote time in your weekly schedule to creativity. Generating creative solutions is like working out a muscle in your brain: the more frequently you use it, the stronger and more effective it becomes.

INTERLUDE—WEWORK, *GET RICH QUICK* COMPANY

WeWork, formally known as the We Company, was founded in 2010 in New York City by Adam Neumann and Miguel McKelvey. Their initial idea was to provide shared workspaces for startups, freelancers, and small businesses, catering to the rise of the sharing economy and a new generation of entrepreneurs.

WeWork's ambitions grew quickly. They ventured beyond just coworking spaces, launching living spaces called WeLive and even starting a private school named WeGrow.

As the shared economy boomed, so did WeWork. It expanded aggressively, and by 2017, WeWork had established itself in fifty-six cities worldwide.

WeWork's meteoric rise was the stuff of business legend, characterized by its grand aspirations and the extravagant lifestyle of its co-founder Adam Neumann.

In 2017, WeWork announced that SoftBank, a major Japanese conglomerate, would be investing $4.4 billion in the company, seemingly validating WeWork's lofty valuation. To commemorate this partnership, Adam Neumann organized an internal event. But instead of the expected business-focused presentation, attendees were in for a surprise.

The event started with Neumann distributing shots of tequila to everyone present. The atmosphere was electric, more reminiscent of a rave than a corporate celebration.

Then, in a move that left attendees bewildered and entertained, Darryl McDaniels from the legendary hip-hop group Run-DMC took the stage to perform. "It's Tricky" blared as employees, still processing the enormity of the SoftBank investment, danced and celebrated.

The irony in the air was so thick you could taste it. It was "tricky." Their incredible $20 billion valuation was based on being classified as a technology company versus a real estate company, drastically bending the numbers in their favor in order to maximize outside investment. It exemplified WeWork's "get rich quick" approach, misleading investors to pour capital into a company built largely on hype.

While, on the surface, this celebratory, tequila-fueled party epitomized a company at its pinnacle, for many, it also highlighted WeWork's exuberant, fast-paced, and often reckless culture.

Rather than adopting a careful, "slow burn" growth strategy, WeWork's core values were about rapid expansion, pushing boundaries, and, as some critics pointed out, occasionally blurring the lines between measured risk and outright arrogance.

This spirit was undoubtedly part of WeWork's charm and initial success. Still, as subsequent events would reveal, a "get rich quick" mentality without a sustainable business model can lead to significant challenges.

A long way from its valuation of $47 billion at its peak in 2019, WeWork suffered a net loss of $696 million in the first half of 2023, struggling to make interest-only payments on its debts.

In November 2023, it filed for bankruptcy, claiming $18 billion in debt and $100 million in unpaid rent, finally admitting defeat after years of deception.

CHAPTER 4

IDEA MINING

"Nowhere can man find a quieter or more untroubled retreat than in his own soul."

—MARCUS AURELIUS

In the previous chapter, I talked about how the abilities to think and create are such high-demand skills because they're so rare, especially given our paint-within-the-lines school system. The person out front, the entrepreneur, of any organization must work to develop the skills of independent thinking and reflection.

The E in RELAX is about "exercising your creativity," creating the habit of developing ideas. In the last chapter, I stressed the importance of reading a variety of strategic sources and hiring a coach. These two activities will give you the seeds of creation, allowing you to start digging into the gold mine that is your mind. They'll provide food for thought to generate ideas of value for your life and business.

Would you like to know the special method I use to maximize my creativity and introspection? Can you guess what it is? I'll give you a hint: it feels like a secret superpower. It's a superpower accessible to almost anyone, though I would guess less than 0.01 percent of the population use it. In this high-tech, app-dominated world we live in, this method will seem so old-fashioned and archaic as to be obsolete, at least at first glance. But it is the most effective habit I have learned and implemented to weather the storms of entrepreneurship for the past decade. Admittedly, I'm not the smartest guy in the room, but this technique gives me a slight edge and allows me to be the person others come to for solutions.

Drumroll...I use voice recorders to capture ideas, to-dos, and reflections. I also record trainings, seminars, and important conversations, as well as coaching calls. Okay, I record virtually everything.

I use simple Sony digital recorders that you can find on Amazon for $30. It's well worth the minimal investment. I usually go through one every quarter or so. They each hold five hundred recordings or four thousand hours of content.

The accountants in the spiritual world say we have sixty thousand thoughts a day.[10] It is very hard to record and categorize the best thoughts and ideas as you go through your day, so sometimes more complicated technology just gets in the way.

The first time I saw one of these recorders used was when I was eighteen years old, working as a grunt for a construction company. I was doing "punch out" work alongside the head foreman of the company.

To this day, I consider that foreman—Fred was his name—to be one of the laziest (well, seemingly laziest) people to occupy a high-level position that I've ever met at any company I have worked for. But it's not quite right to say he was lazy. He

---

10   Wayne W. Dyer, *Wisdom of the Ages: 60 Days to Enlightenment* (New York: Quill, 2002), 2.

worked smart, not hard. He was the right-hand man, second in command, for a home builder in Cincinnati, Ohio, building about fifty new houses per year. They did roughly $10 million in annual revenue. Twenty percent were custom homes; 80 percent were tract homes. We drove around all day, usually smoking copious amounts of pot in Fred's truck, visiting the subcontractors at different job sites, inspecting their work.

Fred never really got out of third gear. He conducted himself in an extremely casual manner, never in a hurry, never stressed out, the opposite of how you would imagine someone in his position might carry themselves. But again, he worked smart. He always had his trusty Sony digital recorder, and he walked around recording five to twenty notes about each property. What needed to be finished or fixed, what needed to be ordered or returned, etc. Everything was recorded. Nothing forgotten.

The following morning, each and every day, at around 6:00 a.m. back at the office, he would write out all the things he had recorded the previous day on a yellow legal pad. He would then arrange them in order of importance, by urgency, and in a way that made logistical sense. It was genius. And everything that needed to get done always got done. Minimal effort was expended.

Since then, I have expanded on Fred's method and made it my own.

Not only do I always carry at least one recorder with me to make sure I capture any fleeting thought or idea that might otherwise escape me, but I also reflect constantly on my current and past ideas—and more often than not, I do so while exercising.

I started carrying my recorders in 2010 while running, and the ideas that came from them slowly but surely advanced me along the courses of my personal and professional lives ever since.

On my runs, I usually carry two recorders with me, one to listen to old ideas and the other to create new ones. I'll listen to a cross section of my recordings from three to six months prior. Each folder holds ninety-nine recordings, so I'll listen to Folder A, recordings one to ten, then Folder B, recordings one to ten, and so on until Folder E. Then I come back around to Folder A again, recordings eleven to twenty, Folder B, eleven to twenty, and repeat the process. Folder A, Recording One, may have been recorded on November 9, 2021, whereas Folder B, Recording Three, may have been captured on December 16, 2021.

The result is that I create a mixing, crossbreeding, synthesizing of thoughts and ideas that effortlessly produces more and better ideas that can be applied to my current problems and circumstances.

For Christmas last year, I bought my baby brother one of these recorders, and he was thanking me within a couple of months. He's a Yale MBA and vice president at a Fortune 500 company. He realized the benefits immediately of this simple tool for recording ideas and thoughts.

Like I mentioned, the average person is said to have sixty thousand thoughts per day. Many of those repeat and run through your mental treadmill all day until they become patterns and form your attitudes.

But a few of them, every day, are new ideas. Thoughts and ideas are short lived, which is why you must record them immediately or they will escape you. The best thoughts always seem to come when we're shaving, showering, or on a road trip, completely disengaged from our work. The easiest way to capture them is to record them on a recorder, avoiding the hassle of having to write them down.

Part of the beauty of bringing the recorders on a run or

when you're exercising is it breaks up your normal thought pattern. When exercising, your biochemistry is primed to a naturally positive state, with endorphins coursing through your body. You can literally direct your mind to dig and think of what you could do to solve your most impactful, lingering problems.

I like to run on the trails throughout the mountains by my house, where I don't see another human being the entire time. My body is able to go into autopilot, and my brain can tap into my subconscious. The subconscious is the key to the treasures of the mind. It holds all the thoughts and memories we've ever had, our "infinite wisdom."

This infinite wisdom is not available to people who live in the hustle and bustle of everyday life. It's not available to those plugged in to the constant chatter coming from their smartphones. It's reserved for people who get away and are able to break their minds free. You must get off your proverbial anthill and up into the ten-thousand-foot perspective to tap into your own divinity. Your divine ability to conjure ideas from your mind or spirit and manifest them into your life.

Infinite wisdom, or divine intelligence, gives you insights into your life that you may not receive otherwise. Ideas bubble up from your subconscious, linking an event from years ago to the present moment. God or the Universe bestows upon you these ideas with some regularity. You will often think of something you heard when you were fourteen years old, combine it with something you learned when you were twenty-four years old, and apply it to your life at age thirty-four.

When you get into the habit of putting the phone away and freeing your mind in this way, it is not uncommon to have a "$100,000 idea" a couple times a month. Most days, I'll have ten to twenty ideas when I'm running, and usually, at least one is a game changer. At least one helps propel my business forward, generate more revenue, or guide me to solve a major problem I've been struggling with.

I do this three times per week so I can tackle and eliminate any persisting problems. If I encounter an uncooperative employee or negative customer headline on a Monday, I'm usually able to work out a solution on my Tuesday run.

Currently, my main business is solar panels and roofing services. We did over $10 million in sales last year. If I ever lost this business and needed to pivot to something entirely different, I have at least a hundred other business ideas I could pursue, all generated from accessing this infinite wisdom on a regular basis.

This is a perfect example of why entrepreneurship means succeeding *on your own terms*. It's why I love being an entrepreneur so much. And it's why, contrary to popular belief, I and others like me are not actually stressed to our eyeballs but rather the opposite: unlike most of the population, we have choices. We can RELAX.

WHY DOES THIS TECHNIQUE WORK SO WELL?

The human mind is a uniquely complex, extremely capable organism. It has been said that it would take at least a billion dollars to reproduce the human mind. It is capable of solving the most complicated of the world's problems, like creating renewable energy sources and sending people to outer space. Yet, most people don't put their mind to use in a productive, creative way.

Everyone has problems. The average person has small problems, and their thoughts are mostly dominated by worry and fear about those problems.

Successful people choose to take on bigger problems. The successful person uses their mind to constantly work out these bigger problems and incrementally improve their life and work.

We can all admit that our thoughts and memories are fleeting, ephemeral flashes in the mind. Most of us can't even remember what we ate for lunch two days ago. We can think of a great idea in the shower about what to add to a presentation that day, but we can't remember it five minutes later when we're drying off. We'll be lying down in bed, trying to go to sleep, and think of that perfect verbiage we should've said to our prospect or coworker earlier in the day. Or we'll be trail running or working out on the elliptical at the gym, and a million-dollar concept will pop into our head. Minutes later, the idea is gone, and we're straining, digging deep into our consciousness, trying to remember this breakthrough that could've changed our life. "It probably would've been as big as the iPod," we tell ourselves, if only we could remember.

Magically, when you get away from the hustle and commit yourself to the practice of freeing your mind, your ideas have a way of coming back to you.

"Idea mining" is what I call my personal method of capturing all my ideas on a digital recorder and then reviewing them constantly to build on them and implement the best ones into my life. Sure, you could use your phone to do the same thing, but your brain works about four times faster than you can write something down or type something into your phone. And if you're using a recorder on your phone and you get a phone call, text, or notification from one of your two hundred apps, it often suspends the recording or becomes a distraction. And your creative process is killed, with your bright idea likely becoming another victim of our attention-deficit world.

I use my recorder for *all* aspects of my life. I record my to-dos, ways I can motivate my sales team, and ideas for new processes. I record my brainstorming of long-term project ideas and plans for networking and recruiting. I record when I contemplate issues that need to be brought up at our weekly and quarterly meetings, how to solve them, and plans for writing and for coaching. I record my thoughts on how to make up with my wife for the latest fight we had. Anything that can help me function at a higher level, I record.

I also mix in recordings of my kids, so when I'm out of town, I have their voices captured. Even if I'm at the office, planning my day, listening to their recorded voices makes me smile.

Idea mining via digital recorder is my single greatest tool. I believe it gives me a huge advantage over my peers. Most times, when facing a difficult conversation, I have already contemplated the solution, working it over during my private reflection time. Slotting time in your daily and weekly schedules for private reflection is crucial to garnering value from your ideas. More on this later.

As often as possible, I also review my recordings and transcribe the wisest thoughts, sometimes acting on them immediately, sometimes filing them away on my Asana or in different folders on my phone.

PEAK STATES PRODUCE THE BEST GOLDEN NUGGETS

The best time to use your recorder, solve problems, and think of ideas is when you're in a peak state. For me, exercising in the morning is a perfect time to get into this peak state and practice idea mining.

When you exercise, your body releases endorphins into your bloodstream. These endorphins trigger a positive, euphoric feeling in your body, similar to morphine. This causes your brain to open the neurotransmitters and allows you to reflect with a positive light on your business and life.

I regularly reflect on the previous day's interactions and conversations during my morning exercise.

Who did I see, what was said, and how did that make me feel?

Did I like the direction that conversation took and the decisions made about that project?

The beauty is that when you're exercising, you rarely frame a problem in a negative light. That's because you are in a state of heightened arousal, which allows your mind to open up and think of solutions, what could have been done better, or what can be improved for next time.

Very frequently, when you're in the heat of the moment, in a discussion with a customer or a management meeting, your brain just isn't relaxed or effective. It's tense. Your ego is up with all its defenses. Your mind doesn't present you with the best words to say or the ability to think of the most advantageous course of action.

The next day, while exercising and reflecting with your recorders, your mind is sharp and relaxed, and you can objectively look back and decide how events from the day before could have been handled more skillfully. Maybe it was an argument with your business partner or your boss, and they are better at thinking on their feet than you. Or they had just had their afternoon coffee, and you were due for yours. Things didn't quite go your way.

Play the tapes and reflect on the previous day. It's a great way to replay the day in your mind and see what you missed.

Where could you have improved?

What meetings can you schedule for tomorrow and with what notes to improve that relationship and get that project going again with everyone's best interests in mind?

What did that client mention on that phone call about an opportunity among the Hispanic population in their hometown? Record that idea. Mark it to revisit if you run out of a fresh supply of leads a month from now.

This is the major leagues of self-development. You will improve yourself and those around you at such a fast pace by using this method that failure is virtually impossible.

Reflecting on what you have recorded in solitude will produce the best results and keep you coming back for more. As scientist and philosopher Blaise Pascal said, "All of humanity's problems stem from man's inability to sit quietly in a room alone."

No one else is there to influence you. You are free from self-conscious judgment as well as the opinions of others, talking away with yourself into your device.

I'll add that using the recorder technique can work at the gym, but gyms tend to contain TVs and people to watch and other distractions that make this practice less effective. Also, people might look at you a little funny. Don't worry, you'll be their employer one day.

DRINK BEER AND WRITE STUFF DOWN

Your idea-mining success does not depend solely on your ability to make the recordings, which is the easy part. It also requires the self-discipline to sit down and reflect on the ideas, evaluate and organize them, and decide which ones to implement into your life or business.

For the first couple years I was using the recorder method, I would accumulate lots of ideas on the devices. But I would resist listening to and organizing the recordings I had made. Sometimes, it would be a month or two before I sat down and reflected on them to garner any value. I dreaded the amount of work I was creating for myself. Oftentimes, I would have two hundred to three hundred ideas to sift through to separate the golden nuggets from the lumps of coal.

This led to the obvious problem that if a good idea was already a month old, it was probably more applicable to my business one month ago. Sometimes, the opportunity had already passed completely.

The point is you must listen to your ideas soon after you capture them and *way* more than once a month. The majority of your ideas, reflections, and strokes of genius will be mission critical within a few days. I promise the economic benefit of this practice far outweighs the pain you must endure to discipline yourself to do it right.

As mentioned earlier, the biggest challenge for me was how to force myself to sit down at my desk for more than a few minutes to complete my "deep" work. Over time, however, I was able to create a kind of Pavlovian conditioning to coerce myself into sitting down at my desk and going through my ideas, deciding which are monetizable now and which can be stored away for the future.

My conditioning is simple. At least two nights a week, usually on Sunday nights, before the week starts, and Wednesday nights, I abandon my family, lock myself in my home office for a couple hours, and reward myself with two or three Bud Lights until the job is complete. Usually after my third Bud Light and two hours of work, I've finished reviewing all my recordings. This routine has become increasingly easier for me over the years, and my wife knows every Sunday and Wednesday night I'm going to make my biweekly pilgrimage upstairs to my home office, and she needs to tend to the kids.

Establishing a routine to review and evaluate your recordings—with an alcoholic beverage or three—at regular intervals will make the task more psychologically sustainable and provide more lucrative results. It becomes an extremely rewarding discipline. The simple act of transcribing your own ideas from a voice recorder will often inspire and help you create new and better ideas, especially when doing so in a relaxed state.

Many times, certain ideas will trigger other more valuable ideas. Oftentimes, around 8:30 to 9:00 p.m., during one of these sessions, I'll generate a $100,000 revelation for the company or a $50,000 solution to a problem our management team has been wrestling with for over a month.

Besides idea mining, you know what else can give you a leg up on your competition? Breaking some rules. I'll tell you why in the next chapter.

CHAPTER 4—ACTION STEPS

- Buy a digital recorder or two. Start recording ideas, thoughts, and to-dos so they no longer escape you in the moment.
- Set times to listen to and reflect on your ideas at least twice a week.
- Organize your thoughts and ideas into Asana or Google Drive, and add urgent items to your daily to-do list.
- Observe how your life and business change for the better using this practice, and decide if it's something you can implement long term.

INTERLUDE—BURT'S BEES, *SLOW BURN* COMPANY

Burt's Bees, known for its natural personal-care products, has a history deeply rooted in humble beginnings and a commitment to organic growth.

The story starts with Burt Shavitz, a beekeeper in Maine who sold honey from the back of his truck. One day, in the early 1980s, he picked up a hitchhiker, Roxanne Quimby, a free spirit interested in a back-to-the-land lifestyle. Together, they formed not just a personal bond but also a business partnership. Initially, they made candles from the leftover beeswax from Burt's honey operation, a sustainable approach to leveraging waste material.

It wasn't until years later that Roxanne stumbled upon a recipe for beeswax lip balm in an old farmer's almanac. Recognizing an opportunity, they created Burt's Bees lip balm, which soon became their best-selling product. While the lip balm quickly gained a reputation for its quality, neither Burt nor Roxanne was tempted to scale up in a way that would compromise their commitment to natural ingredients or sustainable practices. This underscored their "slow burn" philosophy, which became standard procedure for the company as it matured.

Instead of seeking large-scale production or cutting corners with cheaper, synthetic ingredients, the duo insisted on maintaining the natural purity of their goods. They slowly grew their market, maintaining a focus on sustainability and natural ingredients, and added hand creams and lotions to their product line.

Even when the company moved its operations to North Carolina in the mid 1990s and started to experience a surge in growth, it did not succumb to the lure of becoming a "get rich quick" entity. While many companies might have taken shortcuts to meet increasing demand, Burt's Bees stayed true to its roots, meticulously sourcing ingredients and ensuring the same handmade care went into each product.

Burt and Roxanne weren't just selling products; they were selling a philosophy—a return to nature and simplicity. This vision was clear in every product and marketing campaign, differentiating them from competitors.

Burt's personal life, living in a remote cabin and keeping bees, was a testament to his genuine love for nature. This authenticity translated into products that truly represented natural and environmentally friendly values.

Roxanne Quimby was passionate about ensuring the company maintained an ethical stance, from procuring natural ingredients to the business practices they adopted. As the company grew more profitable, Roxanne sold 80 percent of her stake and continued to invest in land for conservation. From 2001–2003, she spent $8 million to buy huge parcels of undeveloped land in northern Maine—nearly sixteen thousand acres in all. This commitment to doing business "the right way" garnered respect and trust from consumers.

Burt's Bees' commitment to being a "slow burn" company paid off. Over time, consumers placed a greater emphasis on natural, ethically produced goods, and Burt's Bees was perfectly positioned to meet this demand. Having already built a reputation for authenticity and quality, the company's consistent approach ultimately led to a buyout for over $900 million in 2007.

In 2016, on the eve of the 100th anniversary of the National Park Service, Roxanne donated 87,500 acres of "awe-inspiring mountains, forests, and waters" in Maine's North Woods to be designated and federally protected as Katahdin Woods and Waters National Monument.[11] The land gift was valued at $100 million and came with a $20 million endowment from Roxanne to support infrastructure development and operations.

In essence, the story of Burt's Bees—from selling honey out of the back of a truck to becoming a global personal-care brand—is a testament to the rewards of patience, authenticity, and staying true to one's values, even in the face of potential rapid profits.

---

11   Office of the Press Secretary, "Fact Sheet: President Obama Designates National Monument in Maine's North Woods in Honor of the Centennial of the National Park Service," press release, August 24, 2016, https://obamawhitehouse.archives.gov/the-press-office/2016/08/24/fact-sheet-president-obama-designates-national-monument-maines-north.

CHAPTER 5

RULES ARE MADE TO BE BROKEN

"The reasonable man adapts himself to the world; the unreasonable one persists in trying to adapt the world to himself. Therefore all progress depends on the unreasonable man."

—GEORGE BERNARD SHAW

While most people would be surprised to hear the word "RELAX" associated in any way with the life of an entrepreneur, I see it differently. Most of us are taught, from the time we are school-aged, to paint within the lines of life. To follow the rules and not make mistakes. "Go to school, study hard, get a good job, and live happily ever after."

Always working within the guidelines of modern civilization, trying to appease our parents, teachers, and bosses, is itself incredibly frustrating and stressful. I'd like to empower you to "leap out of your comfort zone" imposed by the constraints of society by giving you permission to break some rules.

Uber is a great example of how rules are meant to be broken.

In the book *The Upstarts: How Uber, Airbnb, and the Killer Companies of the New Silicon Valley Are Changing the World*, author Brad Stone explains how the old-guard taxi system, in place since the early 1900s, was laughably outdated. With unwieldy amounts of red tape and ridiculous levels of bureaucracy, it did not allow for progress or competition.[12]

In order to launch, survive, and grow in major cities like New York and Los Angeles, the Uber team did not have time to respect all the rules and wait on years-long lists. This meant that founders Garrett Camp and Travis Kalanick and their team went into each new city and essentially ignored all the traditional licensing and regulations. To support the demand they expected with the introduction of their app to each new market, they recruited and deployed a large fleet of vehicles and drivers.

Then, it became a game of cat and mouse between the company and the regulating bodies and local governments of each jurisdiction, with the Uber team repeatedly asking for forgiveness instead of permission—a model they used over and over again in cities around the world, with incredible success.

Imagine if they had gone into each major metropolitan area and asked for permission. First, we would still be waiting, to this day, for the launch of Uber and other rideshare apps in most major cities. Second, their funding would have run out or dried up, and Uber would never have gained any traction as a tech startup. Third, they would never have had the momentum and consumer support it took to successfully set up and then earn forgiveness through petitions and public backing.

By the time the laws were broken and the city and state licensing requirements ignored, Uber had thousands of new

12   Brad Stone, *The Upstarts: How Uber, Airbnb, and the Killer Companies of the New Silicon Valley Are Changing the World* (New York: Littlem, Brown and Company, 2017), 10.

vehicles and drivers in each market. There was enough demand for Uber's services and enough public support that they won major court battles to keep their company afloat and thriving. Uber is now a household name. It has even become a verb, as in, "I'm going to Uber to the concert tonight." Providing service to millions, the company had an astonishing $17.5 billion of revenue in 2021.[13]

According to Richard Branson, "Breaking the rules and challenging convention is in the DNA of every successful entrepreneur."[14] I couldn't agree more. I started my entrepreneurial journey by selling security-alarm systems door to door for two years across the country. The second company I worked for, Pinnacle Security, employed the same strategy as Uber, asking for forgiveness, not for permission.

In the summer of 2009, our little office of twenty-five sales reps sold around three thousand security systems in New Jersey and Dallas, Texas—grossing almost $11 million in revenue. In New Jersey, police officers and other city officials booted us out of forty different municipalities (called "boroughs"). More than once a day, we were forced to find new territory to sell in.

The company had made the decision that pulling permits to sell in each of the small boroughs was going to be too cumbersome and slow. Sometimes, we went through the motions, but many of the municipalities advised us that receiving the permit to sell would take more than a month. By the time the ink was dry on our applications in most places in New Jersey, we weren't even in that state anymore. We had moved on to

---

13   Uber Technologies, Inc., "Uber Announces Results for Fourth Quarter and Full Year 2021," Business Wire, February 9, 2022, https://www.businesswire.com/news/home/20220209005466/en/.

14   Sabian Phippen, "The Richard Branson Interview," *The Worldly Magazine*, February 2015, 12–14, https://issuu.com/theworldly/docs/worldlymag_comp_feb2015_final_versi.

Texas. But we had already sold and installed roughly $4 million of the $11 million we generated that summer.

Multiply that activity times the thirty-plus offices the company had nationwide. Pinnacle Security sold for a cool $70 million to a private equity group a few short years later. Who says you need to follow the rules to make millions in America?

When the COVID-19 pandemic hit, there were quite a few rules put in place that were, let's just say, "unnecessary." Just a few examples include closed playgrounds, closed public parks, and outdoor trails with mask requirements. Now, I'm sorry if you think a virus like that is so contagious you can catch it while hiking up a mountain, but if it were that transmittable and dangerous, we'd be seeing bodies in the streets. Like some sort of zombie apocalypse. Meanwhile, we routinely heard stories of a husband catching a rough case and his wife, who slept in the same bed, never even testing positive for the virus.

The funniest example of this was when I saw a truck full of people driving up one of the trails I run on in California, all thoroughly masked up with their hang-gliding equipment on the top of the truck! They were following the mask requirements, being "safe," and obeying the rules on their way up to *JUMP OFF A MOUNTAIN*! Fascinating.

Regardless of public opinion and the media's incessant fear mongering, my family, especially my mother, was not going to allow my young kids to be barred from playgrounds and public parks for two years. She "channeled her inner Michael" and treated those CLOSED signs as mere suggestions on how to behave, just as I do. She then proceeded to hike the trails without a mask and brought my kids to play on playgrounds or romp around in public parks, uninhibited by silly rules.

My whole life, I have tended to take most rules as suggestions. I was never going to allow some lame-brained rule to ruin my fun. In fact, when I was a kid, I learned pretty quickly that most rules were designed to stifle my fun. NO BUMPING on the bumper cars. NO DIVING in the pool, even in the deep end. FEET FIRST ONLY on water park slides. NO OUTSIDE SNACKS in the movie theaters. I made the decision very early to break and bend these rules as often as possible to create more fun for myself in my childhood and into my adolescence.

My friends and I pushed the limits for years, breaking the rules just to see what we could get away with. "I wonder if we could just stay in the movie theater for a second movie?"

"Yeah, let's try and see."

I'll admit, we unnecessarily took it to the extreme sometimes. "You think you could steal a shirt from Abercrombie & Fitch?"

"Yeah, I think I'll take it into the dressing room and break off the security device."

I'm not proud of it, but I did do that one time and got away with it. The rush was incredible, but it was quickly followed by a week of shame and a vow I would never go to jail for a stupid crime just to prove I could get away with it.

Rules were created by men and women, and, therefore, we have the ability to recreate and bend those rules to fit the changing times. A willingness to understand and apply this principle will help speed up your success as an entrepreneur.

Back to the example of Uber. The changing times demanded a modernized taxi system. The public was sick of the old system; it needed to be overhauled. It just wasn't working for people to have bad service, high fares, and few to no other options. Had Uber waited to obtain the proper licensing, it would have drastically stalled its growth and expansion. Following the outdated rules and regulations, it would've taken Uber ten years to do what it was able to set up in one year. By smashing the old model to pieces and not listening to the authorities, it moved fast and built a company that provides an amazing service to the world.

I'll give an example from my own life. To operate my roofing business in California, the company needs to have a contractor's license. In the state of California, a contractor's license is required to be in business as a contractor. Now, this rule and the California Contractors State License Board were created when most contractors were doing their own work. In 1929. Almost one hundred years ago. The owner-operator of the business was a carpenter or a roofer or an electrician and built their business around themselves. Unfortunately, the owner-operator model is not a sustainable or a scalable one, so most of these companies cannot and do not stay in business very long.

If they are lucky enough to stay in business, they cannot handle the volume of work the market demands; hence, the shortage of capable contractors in California. The companies that actually make it must subcontract out to crews that can handle more volume and have someone at the helm who can run a business, as opposed to a tradesperson.

If you are carrying wood and banging nails all day, when do you have time to sell new contracts? When can you put managers in place to resolve issues with customers or find time to plan how to handle more volume as your company grows?

The list goes on. If you're busy laying shingles on a roof, when will you have time to recruit and hire a foreman to manage the subcontractors? Or train an office administrator to keep track of your accounts receivable? You won't.

I had to figure out a way around this. Following the traditional model, I would've had to work for a contractor for four years then have them sign off on my experience. Bending the rules a bit, I found someone we could pay, first on a per-permit basis then on a monthly salary, to be our license holder. First, "unofficially," and then, eventually, we made it official. We operated unofficially for almost two years, much to the dismay of many of the insurance companies we were collecting hundreds of thousands of dollars from. Ultimately, insurance behemoth Farmers conducted a full-blown investigation and threatened to shut us down. We were forced to make it official at that point.

Had we waited for our business to be "official" to commence operations, I would never have been able to recruit my director of operations (who later became my business partner) or half of the salespeople we had in the business at the time.

You may not be the most popular individual at the time of the rule breaking. The rule-makers and rule-followers will often look down on you with contempt. Travis Kalanick, one of the founders of Uber, has never been the most popular fellow with our critical media. But those same critics are quick to use Uber's service as a faster, cheaper alternative to the old yellow taxi-cabs. Always remember what the famous American author and journalist Mignon McLaughlin said, "Every society honors its live conformists, and its dead troublemakers."[15]

Be prepared to break some rules to make your entrance into business faster and more efficient. Otherwise, you might be forty years old before you can hire your first employee. If you have trouble in your own conscience operating this way, do it in the name of job creation and helping the American economy.

Prohibition in the United States lasted almost fourteen years, from January 1920 to December 1933. Do you think Americans just stopped drinking for fourteen years? Absolutely not. Many daring entrepreneurs got their starts during this time. Those who were willing to break the rules and keep making and sell-

---

15   Mignon McLaughlin, *The Neurotic's Notebook* (Indianapolis: The Bobbs-Merrill Company, 1963), 72.

ing alcohol made a fortune serving the people, despite flying in the face of the law.

You could compare bootleggers and speakeasies during Prohibition to the marijuana shops in Colorado. They bravely operated in defiance of federal law from 2012 until 2020, when it was finally decriminalized. Many fortunes were made during this time, despite marijuana business owners having to launder their money through pizza shops and laundromats.

DUCKS AND EAGLES

Part of breaking the rules is not accepting what people tell you is the normal way of doing business. There are systems and processes most of the world follows that are antiquated and slow.

Waiting is a great way to squander your time away, and time is the most valuable asset we have. Often, in the course of doing business, there is a government authority or tenured bureaucrat you must pass through. This person will appear repeatedly and in many forms. They basically decide their job is more important than your desire to achieve, and they will take their sweet time to slow you down. These people are what I call "ducks."

In this world, there are ducks and there are eagles. Ducks are those people who drift along in their ponds with other ducks, usually staying at the same job for years and complaining about their situation the whole time. They expend the minimum effort required to collect a paycheck and not get fired. You can identify a duck by the slack look on their face and their insistence on following even the silliest rules. You can hear them repeat phrases like, "I'm sorry, sir. It's just our policy. That's just how we do things," never recognizing that there may be a better or faster way.

Then, there are eagles. Eagles advance quickly in their

chosen fields. They fly above the competition and get promoted quickly because they simply find ways to get things done. When they can't advance or when they feel stifled by ignorant bosses or silly bureaucratic rules, they leave. They find someplace where they can excel, or they start their own businesses. You can hear them saying things like, "I'm not supposed to do this, but let me see if I can help you." They find the work-around. They find a better way.

In 2021, we had around sixty roofing permits waiting to be approved by one jurisdiction, the City of San Bernardino. It was January, and the permits had been piling up since November because the pandemic was being used as a convenient excuse for government workers to work even more slowly than they normally do, which is really hard to do.

The chief building inspector, the boss of the Building Department, kept telling us there was nothing he could do. He told our secretary they were backed up and repeated to us daily, "You are just going to have to wait." I didn't consider this an acceptable answer, so I decided to see what I could do to circumvent this particular duck.

I called the City of San Bernardino, bypassing the Building Department, and asked, "Who is the chief building inspector's boss?" I found out, after a series of calls, that the City Director is the person he responds to. The City Director is right below the mayor in the chain of command. After eloquently explaining our problem to his secretary and showing her how important it was to solve, I was put through to the personal line of the City Director. Naturally, this was someone who has made it to his post in life by using some hustle and a "get-it-done" mentality. He was an eagle. He understood our dilemma and helped us with a solution immediately.

With a little bit of research, he discovered most of the permits being held up were more complicated permits that required plans to be approved. Ours were simple re-roofing permits, and there was no reason we should wait in line behind the more complicated projects to get ours approved. In the end, he issued an executive order that all simple permits, including re-roofing permits should be expedited and approved immediately. We had sixty permits—roughly $1.2 million in revenue—approved in a matter of three days, and we proceeded to get caught up on our installation calendar.

This was a big win for us. We got our cash flowing again during one of the most crucial periods of the pandemic, when lots of businesses didn't have the cash flow to keep their doors open.

In your dealings in business, always try to find an eagle who can help you. Don't wait on the ducks. One of the methods I use is asking, "Okay, but who is their boss?" Get to the source as fast as you can, to an eagle who can help you push through to the results you desire.

We deal with insurance companies all day long for the restoration side of our business. There are always several levels of bureaucracy involved before the insurer can approve a large quantity for a claim. Most times, just by asking this question and getting to the real decision-maker, we can shave off a month or two from the time it will take to get paid.

Most everyone, the 98 percent, are programmed to take the path of least resistance, the route that doesn't ruffle any feathers. They will leave something on their boss's desk and wait a month for a response instead of having the difficult conversation of holding their boss accountable to get the job done. If you become the squeaky wheel and do everything you can to get the boss's attention, tasks magically get completed much faster. Oftentimes, months faster.

DON'T BE A SHEEP

The bottom line is you can't continue to be a compliant sheep and succeed in life or business. As you learned earlier, we're trained from the time we are kids to be obedient: get in line, follow the rules, wait your turn, etc. These rules don't work in real life, not as a salesperson, an entrepreneur, or anyone who wants to get ahead.

Unfortunately, being submissive and following all the rules will lead you to a very middle-class, mediocre existence. If you have no other advantages and you weren't born with a silver spoon in your mouth, the reality is you don't have a great head start. There's a lot of competition out there.

You can settle for the life you've lived, probably the same life you grew up with, on the same level of the money pyramid as your parents. It's safe, yes. It will probably provide you with a very comfortable existence. But you've only got one shot, one lifetime.

Why not try for an extraordinary existence with some extra cash in your pocket to live like a rock star? Why not break the boundaries of your comfort zone to achieve freedom from the nine-to-five rat race that almost everyone else is stuck in?

Remember, this is what it's all about: freedom and succeeding on your own terms—and it's why "leap out of your comfort zone" is part of RELAX. The point is you don't always have to accept the norm and muddle along as part of the pack. Becoming a Slow Burn Entrepreneur means exploring some simple strategies to reframe your mentality. Consider ways to break silly rules. Try to work with the eagles and steer clear of the ducks. Then, watch your life transform as you create your own good luck and abundance.

The good news is even if you weren't born with a silver spoon in your mouth, there's a way to get out ahead of the pack:

taking extreme actions to produce extraordinary results, the topic of our next chapter.

CHAPTER 5—ACTION STEPS

- Ask yourself what shortcuts you could take starting today.
- Put together a list of things you could do differently than your parents.
- Think of ways you could serve more people by wasting less time on less important things.
- Ask yourself what risks you can take to forge your own way down the unbeaten path toward successful entrepreneurship.
- Start thinking outside the box—question and challenge your assumptions about how things are supposed to be then create a solution from the ground up.

INTERLUDE—ENRON, *GET RICH QUICK* COMPANY

In 1985, Enron was born from the merger of Houston Natural Gas and InterNorth, a Nebraska pipeline company. During the merger, Enron incurred massive debt and, as the result of deregulation, no longer had exclusive rights to its pipelines.

In order to survive, the company had to come up with a new and innovative business playbook to generate income. Kenneth Lay, who was CEO at the time, hired McKinsey & Co. to assist in developing Enron's new business strategy. It assigned a young consultant named Jeffrey Skilling to the task. Skilling, with his background in banking, proposed an unconventional solution to Enron's revenue and profit woes.

It would create a "gas bank," in which Enron would buy gas from a network of suppliers and sell it to a network of consumers, contractually guaranteeing both the supply and the price and charging fees for the transactions on both ends. Thanks to the young consultant, the company created both a new product and a new model for the industry—the energy derivative.

Lay was so impressed with Skilling's genius that he created a new division in 1990 called Enron Finance Corp. and hired Skilling to run it. Under Skilling's leadership, Enron Finance Corp. soon dominated the market for natural gas contracts, with more contracts, more access to suppliers, and more customers than any of its competitors. With its market power, Enron could predict future prices with great accuracy, guaranteeing consistent profits.

Enron expanded into various businesses, from energy production in different parts of the world to trading a vast range of commodities. The company was seen as a pioneer in the trading of energy derivatives and even ventured into seemingly unrelated sectors like water utilities and broadband services.

In the late 1990s, during the dot-com boom, Enron decided to diversify its portfolio even more and entered into a joint venture with Blockbuster, the movie-rental giant, to provide video-on-demand services. On the surface, this move into the fast-growing digital market seemed strategic. However, the manner in which Enron approached it was far from clever.

While there were many instances of deception and unethical behavior, one of the more absurd moments showcasing Enron's "get rich quick" mentality involved this venture into the entertainment industry.

During one demonstration of their new technology for analysts and investors, instead of displaying a functioning product, they effectively faked the entire presentation. Instead of streaming movies over broadband, as they claimed, they simply had employees behind the curtain start DVD players preloaded with movies in sync with the presenter's commands. It was a smoke-and-mirrors act befitting a company that was later found to be inflating profits and hiding losses.

To make matters even more ridiculous, Enron began claiming "revenue" from this venture almost immediately, even though the service was barely functional and nowhere near ready for a broad consumer release. This premature celebration of an unproven venture was characteristic of Enron's approach—always eager to publicize the next big thing and book imaginary profits rather than methodically build a sustainable business model.

The video-on-demand service quickly collapsed, just like many of Enron's other ill-conceived endeavors.

Enron's downfall is a textbook case of corporate greed and mismanagement. A couple months after a company VP voiced her concerns about Enron's potential to "implode under a series of accounting scandals," the company started to unravel.[16]

On October 16, 2001, Enron announced its first quarterly loss in more than four years after taking losses of $1 billion on poorly performing businesses. Their stock value plummeted, as one analyst reported that the company burned through $5 billion in cash in fifty days. The company filed for bankruptcy protection on December 2, 2001, and the rest is history.

This episode, while just a small piece of the Enron saga, is a humorous illustration of how far the company was willing to go to maintain the facade of success and innovation in its relentless pursuit of quick profits.

---

16   C. William Thomas, "The Rise and Fall of Enron," *Journal of Accountancy*, March 31, 2002, https://www.journalofaccountancy.com/issues/2002/apr/theriseandfallofenron.html.

CHAPTER 6

EXTREME ACTIONS PRODUCE EXTRAORDINARY RESULTS

"A man's wife wants him to be home at 5:00 p.m., she also wants him to conquer the world and be a millionaire, SOMETHING'S GOTTA GIVE."

—Jim Rohn

One of the many observations I've made over the last fifteen years in sales and business is that anytime you can do something and think, "No one else would do this, no one else would go to this extreme," it's probably something you *positively should do*. After all, extreme actions produce extraordinary results. And taking extreme actions to turbocharge your path to success on your own terms is yet another example of what it means to "leap out of your comfort zone."

Taking "extreme action" may seem, on the surface, like the literal opposite of the RELAX mentality, but it's really part of the same thing I keep talking about: stepping into the unlikely sense of calm that comes with, finally, putting trust in yourself and your own autonomous value and power. It's about working smart, not hard. It's about thinking first then taking the action your way, even though your way may not be the "right way." Not doing things how everyone else does them for the sake of conformity, just because that's the way they've been done for years. Exercise your creativity to analyze how the majority is in a rut, and figure out a way to bounce yourself out of that rut.

Every predictable action by a typical person, working 9:00 a.m. to 5:00 p.m. Monday to Friday or being polite and never abrasive, will most likely yield mediocre results. You'll be one of the pack. One of the majority making $70,000 per year, just getting by. Saving for your retirement in thirty years.

This is one of the early epiphanies I had as a young salesman: learn to find ways to go against the grain.

In my first year selling door to door, I noticed most of my brave colleagues would burn themselves out, banging their heads against the wall, trying to sell to people who were home in the early afternoon. Most of the guys would work hard and knock on doors from around 2:00 p.m. to 7:00 p.m. and then be physically and mentally drained and not want to continue working.

I devised a different schedule. I realized if I took a nap in the car from 3:00 to 4:00 p.m., I was easily able to push myself to sell until 9:00 p.m., putting me in front of the most qualified prospects between 7:00 p.m. and 9:00 p.m. The hard-working people with good jobs and good credit. The hustlers who recognized and appreciated my own hustle, working late.

This would inevitably yield me one more sale per day than everyone else. When most guys were selling one alarm a day, I would sell two. Three hundred dollars per commission times about 130 summer selling days per year equals $39,000 in additional annual income. Was it worth it? Absolutely.

According to Tim Ferriss in his book *The 4-Hour Workweek*,

he would make sales calls to businesses from 8:00 to 8:30 a.m. in the morning and 6:00 to 6:30 p.m., before the administrative gatekeepers came into the office and after they left. He would make more sales working four hours a week than all the seasoned veterans making their calls from 9:00 a.m. to 5:00 p.m.

The uninitiated would say, "It's rude to call so early," or "It's bad manners to knock on doors so late at night." Ironically, by continuing to be polite, these poor souls will continue to earn a fraction of what their "rebellious" counterparts do.

Another discovery I made, this time in Texas during the second year of my sales career, was I could make a whole lot more money if I spoke Spanish. My path crossed in the door-to-door sales world with an American guy named John, about my age, who cleaned up on the Spanish sales. I found out he spent a considerable amount of time each year in Colombia. Shortly after, I met a surfer named Nick, another white guy, who surprisingly spoke Spanish as well, successfully making more than half of his sales in Spanish. And sure enough, I came to find out he had spent significant time in Central America, surfing and traveling.

This became a motivating force for me, and I challenged myself to learn Spanish as fast as I could. For two years, I dedicated myself to studying a couple hours a day. I bought Rosetta Stone, hired an online tutor from Colombia, and constantly translated Spanish songs to English. Nothing worked. Two years later, I still struggled to put four words together, let alone an entire sentence.

I could read my sales pitch in Spanish from a sheet of paper, but when someone spoke back to me in their local dialect, I would quickly realize I had an abysmal understanding of the language.

On the recommendation of my friend Nick, I decided to

leave my business in Houston and pursue the long game—learn Spanish by moving to Nicaragua indefinitely. Full immersion was the goal. I was to study in the mornings and surf in the afternoons for as long as it took. On my way to the airport, I dropped my financed car off at the dealership where I bought it. I knew, "No one else will do this. This is pretty extreme."

I ended up spending four months in Nicaragua. I studied three hours every morning at a Spanish language school and spent the rest of the day and most of the night speaking to the locals, practicing what I had learned.

I studied Spanish for four years in high school and spent another two years in independent study, earnestly attempting to learn, to no avail. After spending four months in Central America, I was astonished to see I finally had a strong command of the language. I could now actually hold a conversation, handle a disagreement, or make a convincing argument.

I knew the universe would reward me for my extreme action, and it did, generously.

The years following my life-changing journey to Nicaragua, I was able to double and then triple my income. Not only could I communicate with more customers, my new language skills also opened the door to hiring Spanish-speaking crews to work in my future solar-panel and roofing business.

To this day, my sales team gripes to me about how lucky I am that I speak Spanish. They complain it's not fair that I can talk to the 40 percent of the population who don't speak English in both California and Colorado, where our offices are located.

Little do they know it was an intentional, extreme sacrifice I made at the time, knowing the rewards would be reaped for a lifetime. I routinely encourage them, "Take this winter off, go spend a few months in Central or South America. I promise immersion is the only way to learn."

Unbelievably, in over a decade, no one has taken me up on this challenge, the benefits of which would make you indispensable in any job or industry almost anywhere in the United States. In my humble opinion, learning a second language should be mandatory for anyone trying to make it in our country in sales, business, or otherwise.

THE GRASS MAY BE GREENER

Always keep your eyes wide open to determine if you can find other opportunities within your chosen field or spot a niche market you could take advantage of coming on the horizon.

Typically, entrepreneurs will stay loosely in their own knowledge zones when it comes to choosing a business to pursue and grow. I don't want to discourage this. If you have some sort of advanced or proprietary knowledge in a certain field, the grass is not always going to be greener in another field. Paul Angone, author of *101 Secrets for Your Twenties* says, "The grass is always greener on the other side, until you get there and realize it's because of all the manure."[17] Meaning, all businesses have their downsides, so you can stop trying to find the perfect one. Remember, just as you are evaluating someone else's lot in life and wishing you were in their line of work, there is someone wishing they were in yours.

But if you don't have the expertise or aren't equipped to exploit a certain opportunity, you may need to determine if there's another more profitable side of your business you could pursue.

I'll give you an example. When I was first in the roofing and roof-restoration business in 2013 and 2014, I realized the

---

17   Paul Angone, *101 Secrets for Your Twenties* (Chicago: Moody Publishers, 2013).

competition was getting a bit crowded. The hail, or "diamonds from the sky," that would fall every year attracted more and more competition to the Denver, Colorado, area, where I was based. It got to the point where literally thousands of companies became like vultures, swarming the same hail-affected neighborhoods to get their piece of the pie. And this happened after each and every severe weather event.

I became aware that this opportunity wasn't sustainable. The profitability had to decrease based on the sheer number of companies willing to work in the same market and industry. And sure enough, it did decrease.

It was a simple supply-and-demand equation for the insurance companies. More supply of roofers, less demand for the *quality* roofers who require higher prices. The competition drove prices down to what insurers were willing to pay, eventually squeezing away the profit margins.

I kept my eyes open and made an interesting observation. For every twenty roofing companies in each hail-affected neighborhood, there was one rogue company in the area selling solar. I discovered this was a new, disruptive industry, with technology that most people knew nothing about.

Slowly, over about a year, I investigated whether I could generate the same income in the solar industry as I did in roofing. More importantly, was the change worth the risk?

In her book, *Stop Playing Safe*, Margie Warrell wrote, "Your brain is wired to avoid risk. Not only does it naturally exaggerate the potential consequences of failure, but it underestimates your ability to handle them."[18]

I forged ahead. I talked to friends in the industry who were operating in California, the pioneers of the solar industry, and

---

18   Margie Warrell, *Stop Playing Safe* (Melbourne: John Wiley & Sons Australia, 2013), 34.

found I could realistically double my income by making the jump to solar.

Partnering with an old friend, we moved to California and took the plunge into the budding renewable-energy industry.

The timing couldn't have been better.

In the first forty years of the mainstream production of photovoltaic (PV) solar, 1975 to 2016, around fifteen gigawatts of solar were installed in the United States. In 2016, my second year in the industry, fifteen gigawatts were installed in a single year.[19]

The amount of solar installed in that one year was equivalent to the previous forty years combined. Our company was able to sell almost $2 million of solar the year we launched and close to $4 million in our second year. Bingo!

Inevitably, within three years, companies caught on to the sickening profitability of the solar industry in California. Before we knew it, every contractor was a solar professional. Not only roofers and electricians, as you would expect, but even plumbers and handymen had jumped into the game.

We had to figure out a way to differentiate ourselves again. I started noticing that around 30 percent of the solar jobs we were slated to install got kicked back in the eleventh hour, right before the installation date. The majority of the houses in our area were built between 1940 and 1970 and still had their original roofs. Our site survey technicians, reviewing the roofs, were finding major issues, including three layers and wood shake roofs underneath the shingles, making it impossible to install solar.

Robert Kiyosaki in his *Rich Dad* books often says, "Cynics

19   Robert Margolis, David Feldman, and Daniel Boff, "Q4 2016/Q1 2017 Solar Industry Update," Sun Shot, U.S. Department of Energy, April 25, 2017, chrome-extension://efaidnbmnnnibpcajpcglclefindmkaj/ https://www.nrel.gov/docs/fy17osti/68425.pdf.

criticize, and winners analyze."[20] Successful people understand that an unfair advantage exists. Most people in my position would have left the market entirely, and many did, opting to continue with solar and staying away from the less sexy roofing profession. Anticipating an opportunity, I decided to pull the trigger and hire a marketing company to give us a presence online as a roofing business. This was three years before we were even licensed to install roofs.

A few leads trickled in every month due to the strong Santa Ana winds that came through, causing damage to thousands of roofs. A handful had already been paid out on insurance claims for wind damage to their roofs. Most who had wind damage had no idea they could use their insurance money to pay for the roof replacements.

The light bulb went off again. Is there a way to combine insurance restoration roofing—popular in Colorado and Texas—with our solar business in Southern California? It looked like this new business model might be feasible and unique to our area and market.

This is when we joined our current insurance restoration roofing business in Southern California with our photovoltaic solar business. We became, and still are to this day, one of the only companies in this niche in Southern California. We are able to obtain free roofs for our customers, paid for by their homeowner's insurance, and then help them save thousands with solar as well.

There is a misconception among young entrepreneurs that they must radically change what they're doing to hit it big. That somehow there is a revolutionary alternative that will be their

---

20   Robert T. Kiyosaki, *Rich Dad Poor Dad: What the Rich Teach Their Kids about Money—That the Poor and Middle Class Do Not* (New York: Business Plus, 2010), 199.

jackpot to becoming the next unicorn business, like Tesla or Amazon.

The reality is that far less than 1 percent of startups actually evolve into a unicorn startup (over $1 billion valuation), like Uber, Airbnb, Slack, or Stripe. And Uber and Airbnb each took on over a billion dollars of debt in order to achieve this kind of growth![21]

The Slow Burn Entrepreneur doesn't buy into the "get rich quick" myth that the media tries to sell us. Yes, it's a sexier story to imagine the billionaire tech entrepreneur breezed his way to the top. But look deeper into their stories. How often are they ignoring the ten to fifteen years of sweat and blood, trial and error that it took to make every "overnight" success?

I've seen some of my friends bounce between completely unrelated industries every few months, trying to find the pot of gold at the end of the rainbow. They are attempting to become the next Elon Musk or Jeff Bezos, when in reality, there are hundreds of levels of innovation. And at each level, thousands of thriving millionaires are being produced.

You don't need to create a drastic change or a major innovation.

Roofing and solar are very similar trades. Knowledge in one easily translates to the other. It didn't take rocket science to discover this window of opportunity. But it did take some reflection on how to challenge the status quo.

I have a rule in my own life. Every two years, I need to revisit what I'm doing and determine if it's what I want to continue doing.

---

21 Kyle Stanford, "Here's Why the Biggest Unicorns in the World Are Taking on Billions in Debt," PitchBook, June 16, 2016, https://pitchbook.com/news/articles/heres-why-the-biggest-unicorns-in-the-world-are-taking-on-billions-in-debt.

If it's not, I make a decision. Is there a sensible way to reca-librate and move the company in a slightly different direction? Or is there an unorthodox path we can take to get marginally out ahead of the curve?

You've learned that one way to get ahead is to leap out of your comfort zone and take extreme actions that most wouldn't consider. In the next chapter, we'll talk about how to make getting out of your comfort zone a daily habit.

CHAPTER 6—ACTION STEPS

- Think of some extreme actions you could take to speed up your success. These actions may feel like a step backward in the short term but will often bring exponential returns in the long term.
- Instead of thinking about pivoting 180 degrees to make a positive change in your business, think about how you can pivot 15 degrees. Use your expertise, and expand outward, slightly, to explore new opportunities and gain more market share.

INTERLUDE—CHICK-FIL-A, *SLOW BURN* COMPANY

Chick-fil-A's founder, S. Truett Cathy, and his brother Ben opened a small diner called the "Dwarf Grill" in Hapeville, Georgia, in 1946. This diner served a variety of food items, including hamburgers. In the early 1960s, Cathy noticed that most fast-food restaurants didn't serve a chicken sandwich because the process of cooking the chicken was too time consuming and often led to a dry, greasy, or bland product. He remembered that his mother cooked fried chicken with a heavy top to trap in the heat and moisture. This inspired Cathy to try to cook a boneless chicken breast in a pressure fryer (a type of pressure cooker). He discovered the chicken was ready to eat in the same time it took to grill a hamburger and it retained much of its moisture and flavor without the greasiness imbued by most traditional methods.

Once he had the method, he needed a recipe for the perfect chicken sandwich. A man known for his innovative spirit, Cathy became determined to create a better chicken sandwich that was more flavorful and tender than what was available at competitor fast-food restaurants. He began experimenting with different recipes in his own kitchen, trying to perfect the flavors and texture. He would try different breadings and spice mixtures and ask customers at his diner to taste different combos and provide feedback. After numerous attempts and adjustments, he eventually came up with a unique recipe that featured a boneless, hand-breaded chicken breast flavored with more than twenty seasonings served on a soft, buttered bun with pickles.

Cathy's new chicken sandwich was a hit with family and friends, and he decided to introduce it at his first Chick-fil-A restaurant at Greenbriar Mall in Atlanta, Georgia, in 1967. The "A" in the name represents the "Grade A" quality chicken used in its sandwiches. The response from customers was overwhelmingly positive, and the sandwich quickly gained popularity.

One distinctive aspect of Chick-fil-A's business model is its commitment to remaining closed on Sundays. Truett Cathy, a devout Southern Baptist, made the decision from the beginning to keep all Chick-fil-A locations closed on Sundays to allow employees to attend church and spend time with their families.

Chick-fil-A's commitment to being a "slow burn" company is exemplified by its unique approach to franchisee selection. It is known for having one of the strictest selection processes in the fast-food industry. In fact, it is harder to become a Chick-fil-A franchisee than it is to get into Harvard. Chick-fil-A only accepts roughly 115 franchisees from the forty thousand applications it receives every year. That means only 0.25 percent of applicants are chosen compared to Harvard's 3.5 percent acceptance rate.

Unlike many other fast-food chains, which rapidly expand by awarding franchises to the highest bidders, Chick-fil-A takes a patient and highly selective approach. The company's leadership has stringent requirements and firmly believes in finding people who embody the brand's principles and customer-centric philosophy rather than solely focusing on financials.

One particularly famous example of this approach occurred when a celebrity, a well-known musician, approached Chick-fil-A with interest in opening a franchise. This individual had the financial resources to meet the company's criteria, but during the application process, it became apparent their values did not align with Chick-fil-A's commitment to family, community, and providing exceptional service.

Despite the potential for increased publicity and profit that could come from partnering with a celebrity, Chick-fil-A chose to decline the application. This decision underscored the company's unwavering commitment to its values and long-term vision, even at the cost of a "get rich quick" opportunity.

Chick-fil-A's "slow burn" approach, emphasizing cultural alignment and long-term values over quick financial gains, has been a fundamental part of its success. It maintains the integrity of its brand and culture, even in the face of potentially lucrative opportunities.

Chick-fil-A's revenue in 2022 was an astonishing $6.37 billion, more than $8.5 million per store, the best numbers by a long shot in the fast-food industry.

CHAPTER 7

PUSH YOUR COMFORT ZONE LIMITS, EVERY DAY

"Move out of your comfort zone. You can only grow if you are willing to feel awkward and uncomfortable when you try something new."

—BRIAN TRACY

The sobering reality is that *Forbes* reports that 70 percent of all new businesses fail within ten years. Twenty percent fail in the first year, 30 percent in the second year, 50 percent by year five, and the decline continues until a full 70 percent of businesses have failed within the first ten years of their existence.[22]

In the face of stats like that, you're probably wondering how on earth I can still be talking about "Slow Burn Entrepreneurs," success on your own terms, and the RELAX method. But I stand by everything I've said, and here's why.

---

22   Laura Cowan, "Eight Common Reasons Small Businesses Fail," *Forbes*, October 24, 2019, https://www.forbes.com/sites/ellevate/2019/10/24/eight-common-reasons-small-businesses-fail/?sh=769294124fbb.

Being a "Slow Burn Entrepreneur" means not putting an arbitrary, stress-inducing timeline on your business success. Just like all the other most meaningful parts of life, like your health, marriage, and family, staying in the game is the most important factor. It means accepting that everything you need to go through is just part of the ride. Enjoy it, embrace it, even. If during part of the ride, you experience some failure, just know it happened for a reason. It all works out if you don't quit. Let it serve you, not hurt you. The only way a failure can hurt you is if you stay down, sulking in self-pity. Get back up, try it a different way. Try something new.

The thick skin you'll develop by pushing your comfort-zone limits will allow you to take tough times in stride. The prospect of failure won't have that same paralyzing effect on you when you've spent time programming your mind, recognizing your value, and exercising your creativity. You know there is always another opportunity around the corner for someone with your skill set. Entrepreneurs, those who experience the magic of finding success on their own terms, don't fear failure. They RELAX.

Nevertheless, failures will be some of the most uncomfortable situations you'll face in business. So why try? Why put yourself through this inevitable pain?

Because each failure can be an invaluable learning experience. A mistake you won't make again. If you're reading this book, I have no doubt you'll use your small interim failures as stepping stones to become one of the 20 percent who succeed in the long term. The 20 percent who reflect and make the necessary adjustments to push through to success.

This is why you must practice getting uncomfortable. Discomfort and rejection are feelings you will grow accustomed to. It's better to practice feeling them when the stakes are low.

The following are some of the ways I've learned to practice getting uncomfortable.

"CAN I ASK YOU A HUGE FAVOR?"

Get in the habit of asking for favors. I like to use the line, "Can I ask you a *HUGE* favor?" And it doesn't matter if I'm asking for straws for my kids' lemonade at a restaurant or an investor to read a business plan. It's an attention getter. It makes people perk up and listen so you have their undivided attention. And believe it or not, people love doing favors for others.

There are a few ways you can easily practice getting people to do you favors.

The first way is asking to jump ahead in lines. I routinely do this at the grocery store. If I only have to pick up a couple items, it doesn't matter what time of day, I will make sure I don't wait in any of the grocery lines. "Huge favor to ask, do you mind if I go ahead of you, I've only got these two items? Great, thank you, I appreciate it." Smile. Wink. At the same time, I'm assuming they will allow me to pass ahead of them, and I move in the direction of the front of the line. Time is our most precious asset, don't judge me.

Sounds simple, but you'd be surprised at the number of people who will stand behind a family with a full cart of groceries holding a single item in their hand. Meanwhile, the minutes of their life tick away, patiently waiting, being a good citizen of the world, another sheep in the herd.

The second way, one that's not used often enough in our selfie-obsessed culture, is asking someone to take your photo. Even if it's just you and your child on a hike or in a public area, get out of your comfort zone and ask someone to do you the "huge favor" of snapping your photo. The more you do this, the easier it becomes to ask for real favors in life and business.

The third way is how I make my sales people get out of their comfort zones and ask for favors. I still go out door-knocking with them once or twice a week and use this tactic almost every time. Fifteen years ago, when I was starting in door-to-door sales, they would drop us off, tell us to take three streets, and stay there from 1:00 p.m. to 9:00 p.m. If we needed to use the bathroom or eat, we had to figure it out.

One way we survived was by asking friendly homeowners to use the restrooms inside their houses. As I'm finishing up a house visit, I'll say, "Last thing, before I go, can I ask you a huge favor? Do you mind if I use your restroom real quick?"

Every time I do this with a new rep, it always amuses me to hear them gasp or giggle a little bit because they think I'm joking. "What? You're going to use a stranger's bathroom, and you just knocked on their door fifteen minutes ago? They don't even know you!" But it's a great challenge to expand your comfort zone and get accustomed to asking for uncomfortable things.

When I was starting the roofing side of my company and needed a contractor's license, I had to ask the "huge favor" of a friend's brother to read my business plan and consider becoming our license holder. This man was semi-retired, spending half his time serving missions for his church in Central America. It took a few meetings and "being the squeaky wheel" for him to sit down, read the business plan, and finally agree to lend us a helping hand. As mentioned earlier, we set up a win–win situation that allowed him to be paid on a per-permit basis and then, later, a monthly salary to become our unofficial license holder. Using his license, we were able to break into the roofing-restoration market in Southern California, installing $20 million in roofs in our first five years. And it all started by asking for a favor.

PUBLIC SPEAKING MAKES ME PUKE

As we've talked about, budding entrepreneurs must step out of their comfort zones every day in order to continually taste success. In order to boost their confidence and show themselves they can do it. Yes, I said "step," not "leap"—that's what these daily practices are about, they are not our extreme actions. It's about routinely pushing the envelope, stepping outside your feeling of safety, your personally induced boundaries, and, little by little, expanding your comfort limits.

If you are in your twenties or early thirties when starting your career in sales or business, you will have to convince adults—intimidating, responsible adults—to follow you and your ideas. This alone can be paralyzing for the great majority of people I've trained in sales, prompting them to quit after their first day of training.

The lucky few make it past their first day of intimidating office training, with lots of role play and pressure in the "hot seat." However, the fear that most people feel on their first day in the field, in front of real, warm-blooded human beings, is enough to have them throw in the towel.

You must embrace this fear constantly and step out of your comfort zone. As your comfort zone expands, your business will expand as well.

My Achilles' heel in business, my limiting factor, has always been my lack of ability, or complete unwillingness, to engage in public speaking.

"Lack of ability" is putting it lightly. For the first twenty-five years of my life, I was terrified anytime I was required to stand up in front of a group. I avoided speech making or any sort of leadership like the plague.

To this day, I remember the source of my phobia. I was forced to give a speech in third grade for Black History Month about the life and achievements of Booker T. Washington. We were each assigned a ten-minute slot, and I was not prepared. I had finished the paper for the speech just hours before my presentation was scheduled, earlier that morning. I had waited so long because instinctively I knew putting off the preparation for the presentation (writing the paper) put off the nerves just a little bit longer.

When it came time for me to speak, I got up in front of my class with my poorly prepared notes, and I froze. A few eternally long seconds later, I finally got into it, trying not to make eye contact with the teacher or anyone in the class.

I proceeded to turn bright red. Sweat dripped from my forehead and seeped from my prepubescent armpits through the entirety of the talk. Seven agonizing minutes later, I looked like I had run a 5K race at a full sprint. My psychological revulsion to getting up in front of a group to speak had manifested itself in a crippling physical reaction.

The teacher thanked me politely, and I received a pity golf clap from my classmates. I excused myself to the bathroom, where I took a good fifteen minutes to "cool down" from this horrible, humiliating first public-speaking experience.

Public speaking is also the reason I ultimately dropped out of college. I had barely made it through four years at Ohio State and was taking my last few business classes at the University of Hawaii—Manoa. One was a higher-level communications class with a charismatic grad-student teacher. We were all forced to sit in a circle and face each other, as we would in future boardroom meetings, to debate different business topics.

All eyes were on me each time I spoke, and I hated it. I was having constant anxiety attacks where I would turn beet red. Sweating profusely, just like during my episode in third grade, I would routinely have to excuse myself mid-class to go splash cold water on my face in the bathroom.

I was so tired of dealing with these episodes, I decided to drop out of school entirely. I would, as you know, become a beach bum on the North Shore of Oahu, where I could steer clear of professional situations altogether.

Little did I know one short year later I would be thrust into professional selling, where presenting and having all eyes on me was going to become an inescapable hourly routine.

In early 2010, I was asked to give sales training for the first time. I had become the statewide sales leader and was invited to do some training in front of the veteran salespeople, many twice my age. The audience wasn't very large, maybe fifteen to twenty people, but it was extremely intimidating because these were adults, and I was still a kid in my eyes.

This was during the brief period when I was selling insurance because my girlfriend at the time did not want me selling door to door across the country. Looking back, I don't blame her.

I got all dressed up in a button-down shirt and slacks, ready to teach a little bit about what I was doing to convert the large percentage of sales I was closing. In the previous months, I had realized virtually "overnight" success with this company. But that success didn't help calm my nerves.

My anxiety took over, my body forced me to stop driving, and I proceeded to blow chunks in a gas station toilet a mile from the office. I continued on, nailed the training that day, and promised myself I wouldn't be doing any more of those "damn trainings" for at least another year.

Let me add that, at the time, I only owned one nice dress shirt, which I wore to all our important sales meetings. The day after I gave this training, I was at another company-wide gathering at the headquarters in North Carolina. I kept wondering, "Who smells like puke?!" I found myself literally looking around for a couple hours during the meeting to find the culprit. I finally realized I was wearing the same shirt as the night before. Apparently not everything had gone into the toilet at the gas station, and I was wearing the same puke-stained shirt from the day before. Gross.

Through 2011 and 2012, I forced myself to continue building sales teams, which required giving sales trainings almost every day, even though it was still extremely uncomfortable for me every time. I routinely forced myself to address my fear head on by getting up in front of the class every day.

I attended more than a hundred Toastmaster meetings to practice public speaking to strangers. I knew if I didn't stay out of my comfort zone, I would slip back into it and continue as a sales rep, never building anything for myself or my family.

The comfortable choice would have been to just continue selling solo and not force myself to experience the discomfort and challenge that public speaking always poses for me.

Instead, I subjected myself to leading sales trainings two to three times a week at a minimum. Once a week, I would give a longer new-hire class, usually lasting three to four hours at a time. I knew I was progressively becoming more comfortable and evolving into a skilled speaker, which is invaluable as an entrepreneur.

Warren Buffett, consistently one of the richest men in the world, talks about how, early in his career, he would become physically ill before giving speeches.[23] But he knew he had to become comfortable with this skill to succeed in business. He enrolled in a Dale Carnegie public speaking course when he was in his early twenties to overcome his fear. They met once a week over a period of a few months. Buffett came to realize

---

23 "Bloomberg Billionaires Index," *Bloomberg*, last modified April 21, 2024, https://www.bloomberg.com/billionaires/.

that everyone else in the class was just like him: just as fearful of public speaking, stuttering and freezing in front of the class just like he did. Young Warren finished the twelve-week course feeling more confident and transformed into someone who enjoyed speaking to strangers.

To this day, despite having degrees from the University of Nebraska and Columbia, he lauds that Dale Carnegie public speaking course as the best education he ever received. The "Oracle of Omaha" realized that no matter what you do, you'll have to speak in front of people and convince others of your ideas. So, he committed to pushing his comfort zone until he became comfortable with this invaluable skill.

The majority of Americans fear public speaking more than death itself. If it scares you, you're not alone. But you need to get over it to be a successful entrepreneur.

Entrepreneurs are leaders. They are out in front. Leaders must speak in front of groups to convey ideas and influence their employees. To disagree or deny this fact would be naive.

You may have some of the greatest ideas in the world, but they're worthless if you can't communicate them to others. As business philosopher Jim Rohn said, "It's hard to find a rich hermit."[24]

Toastmasters is the best organization I've found to get the nerves out and practice public speaking. They meet once a week, they're very welcoming, and everyone is coming for the same reason: they're nervous and want to tame their anxiety while speaking to groups.

You'll realize very quickly that you're not alone. Most clubs will not make you speak the first time you show up, except to quickly introduce yourself. I attended Toastmasters meetings

---

24   Jim Rohn, *The Treasury of Quotes* (Irving, TX: Jim Rohn International, 1994), 86.

for almost an entire year before I mustered the guts to stand up and give a speech.

As I gave more and more speeches, I learned to channel my adrenaline-charged fear. I would pretend that my fear was merely "excitement," and that excitement would carry me through my speeches with enthusiasm and energy. I will admit, to this day, I still feel this "excitement" when the group I'm speaking to is larger than ten or fifteen people, but it is under control. I can effectively deliver my message, the audience stays engaged, and I can convince others of my ideas.

It never feels easy to deliver a message to strangers, or to peers for that matter. Not the first time or the hundredth time. Keep doing it. Repetition is the best cure for fear. Feel the fear, acknowledge it, then do it anyway, again and again. Eventually, it becomes a fun challenge you look forward to.

THAT'S A BEAUTIFUL HOUSE, WHAT DO YOU DO FOR A LIVING?

My dad was a chemical engineer for forty years before he retired. Whenever we'd go anywhere nice, he'd always ask himself out loud in our minivan, "What do all these people do for a living to afford these houses?" I'd always say, "Let's stop and ask them." We never stopped and asked.

This was typically followed by some negative, cynical comment from my mom or dad: "They're probably robbing the little guys," or "They're definitely part of the mafia to be able to afford a house here."

I always thought to myself, *I doubt all of these people are bad people. There can't be that many bad people in the world.*

I've made it a practice to find out what "these people" do for a living. Anytime I go anywhere fancy or affluent, I run along the beach, and I stop and ask anyone outside, "What *do you do* for a living?" If they say they are retired, I ask, "What *did you do* for a living?"

This is a great comfort challenge. These people are usually extremely wealthy, sometimes intimidating, and you are often trespassing on their property. Don't stress it; you are an innocent jogger out for your morning run. Surprisingly, if you actually do this, you'll find out firsthand they're some of the nicest people in the world. Most will stop their gardening or reading and talk to you for half an hour. They'll tell you their life story if you have the time to listen.

Funny side note: when I was with my dad in my youth, we never stopped and talked to these people. Then, recently, my dad bought a boat. Now, I can actually convince him to stop and talk to the people around his condo while we're cruising around the canals of Naples, Florida.

"I was an investment banker." "I own my own real estate brokerage." "I owned a printing business." "I own a computer hardware company." "I invented the pacemaker." "I was a distributor for Budweiser."

Most of the successful people you will talk to are entrepreneurs and business owners in some regard. The investment bankers and inventors of the world are often employed by big companies but ultimately work for themselves.

The cream of the crop, the top 2 percent who own the most amazing real estate in the world, are business owners. It's a great affirmation of why we do what we do. Why being an entrepreneur is the greatest game in the world.

I still talk to people on my jogs, just to make sure I stay out of my comfort zone at all times and to reinforce my belief that owning your own business is the best way to live in this life.

FEAR OF HEIGHTS? GO JUMP OUT OF A PLANE

I was strapped to the front of an ex-Marine. The single-engine plane clacked upwards, climbing from the Dillingham Airfield up above the Pacific Ocean. We were slated to jump out in a few short minutes. Everything below became smaller and smaller, fading into patterns of green and blue patches that made up the stunning North Shore of Oahu.

For as long as I could remember, I had wanted to try skydiving, and I had finally worked up the courage to try it out. At this moment, I was second-guessing myself, wondering why we were about to jump out of a perfectly good airplane.

I tried to convince myself inside my own head, *This plane is not that great…we should jump out of it…we're safer outside this aircraft.*

Everyone was quiet as we reached the fourteen-thousand-foot mark. "Jumpers ready!" Each pair of jumpers scooted to the front of the plane, where we readied ourselves to jump. One by one, the pairs jumped out and were swooshed away into the blue abyss. It was my turn. I was so nervous I closed my eyes, held my breath, and grasped my chest straps. My instructor yelled, "HEAD UP! STEP OUT!" and we plummeted toward the turquoise blue of the Pacific Ocean.

The fear was behind me instantly, and I was overcome by a full-body adrenaline rush and bliss like I had never experienced. After forty-five seconds of speeding toward the earth, we pulled the ripcord, and the parachute shot out above us. We drifted down the last mile out of the heavens, drinking in the intoxicating views of the majestic coastline.

I wondered, *Is this what I was afraid of all those years?*

A few months after my first skydiving adventure, I returned to do it again. This time, I tipped the instructor beforehand to do a pair of backflips right as we jumped out of the plane. It was incredible.

A couple years later, I took a death-defying mule ride into the Grand Canyon. For those with a fear of heights, try this as your ultimate challenge. I promise it's more terrifying than skydiving.

Recently, I ran and jumped off a mountain in California, paragliding thousands of feet down to the valley floor.

Much like public speaking, I faced my fear of heights by confronting it head on. You must routinely do the thing you fear to keep the fear at bay. To keep it from paralyzing you. To show yourself that your mind is stronger than fear. That most fears are just overworked excitement, our lizard brain telling us to flee from scary things.

For as long as I can remember, I have been afraid of heights. Anytime I'm more than two stories up and I look down, even if it's through a window, my knees get weak and my stomach gets queasy. Nevertheless, in my mid-twenties, I realized it was important for me to do the things I fear. I knew I would be missing out on plenty of thrills if I allowed my fear to hold me back.

Being a roofing contractor now, you would think I would be comfortable on roofs. I'm not. It's still just about as scary as it was the first time. During my inaugural summit of a two-story roof, more than a decade ago, I took my shoes off and crawled onto it, gripping it like a cat. I don't need to take my shoes off anymore, that would be embarrassing, but I do feel the fear and approach it with caution, then I proceed anyway.

You must feel the fear, acknowledge the emotion, and ask yourself, "Is the reward greater than this emotion I'm feeling? What happens if I let my fear hold me back and don't take this action? What will I miss out on? How great would it be if I could tell my lizard brain to chill out for a second so I can do this life-changing, exciting adventure that may lead to more experiences and opportunities?"

Life is too short to allow your actions to be dictated by fear. Say what you want about Elon Musk, but you have to respect the sheer quantity of innovation he's managed to accomplish in his lifetime, from peer-to-peer banking with PayPal to electric cars at Tesla and now space travel with SpaceX. In his recent biography by Walter Isaacson, Elon's cousins, the Rive brothers (founders of SolarCity), talk about how Elon, in his younger days growing up in South Africa, prided himself on being the most fearless among the group.[25]

Elon talks about feeling the fear and acting anyway in an interview he participated in for YCombinator in 2016. Speaking with Sam Altman, he said, "People shouldn't think, 'I feel fear about this and therefore I shouldn't do it.' It's normal to feel fear... When something is important enough, you believe in it enough, that you do it in spite of fear."[26] Amen, Elon.

Remember, part of the magic of being an entrepreneur is the ability to program your own mind. It's how you came to "recognize your value." Now, I call on you to apply this tool—routinely stepping out of your comfort zone—to get over the things you fear most on your own terms.

In this chapter, you've learned you must do the things you fear most to empower yourself to be a bigger and better person and business leader. Next, we'll look at ways to shore up your mental fortitude by creating a morning routine.

---

25 Walter Isaacson, *Elon Musk* (New York: Simon & Schuster, 2023), 25.

26 Lisa Calhoun, "When Elon Musk Is Afraid, This Is How He Handles It," Inc., September 20, 2016, https://www.inc.com/lisa-calhoun/elon-musk-says-he-feels-fear-strongly-then-makes-this-move.html.

CHAPTER 7—ACTION STEPS

- Work on your public speaking by finding the closest Toastmasters to your home or office, and attend every week you can.
- Volunteer to lead a meeting or give a company training next week.
- Talk to three people who are more successful and/or wealthier than you. Walk or run along the beach (or lake) in the wealthiest area of the town you live in. Start a conversation. The first time will be super uncomfortable and awkward. Who cares?
- What do you fear most? Make a quick list.
- Think of what makes your stomach jump into your throat. Now, go do that thing. Go skydiving. Go SCUBA diving.
- Take the action that makes you most nervous or scared so you will be more prepared and empowered to take on whatever other challenges come up in your entrepreneurial journey. They will feel like a piece of cake.

INTERLUDE: WEBVAN, *GET RICH QUICK* COMPANY

Webvan was founded in 1996 by Louis Borders, the co-founder of Borders Books. The company's mission was ambitious: to revolutionize the grocery delivery industry by allowing customers to order groceries online and have them delivered to their doorsteps. Webvan quickly gained attention and secured substantial funding.

With the dot-com bubble in full swing, Webvan went public in November 1999, raising $375 million in one of the most significant IPOs at the time. The company used this capital to aggressively expand its operations, entering multiple US markets.

Webvan's rapid expansion into several markets suggested a degree of impatience. Instead of methodically testing and refining its model in one area before moving to the next, it operated with a "land grab" mentality common in the dot-com era, fearing it'd miss out if it didn't scale quickly.

Webvan's leaders seemed to believe that with enough capital, they could overcome any obstacle. This mindset led to huge investments in infrastructure and technology, perhaps under the presumption that throwing money at problems would automatically result in solutions.

Grocery delivery, given its logistical intricacies and thin margins, is complex. Webvan's leadership may have underestimated these complexities, especially concerning supply chain management and the perishable nature of many products.

In its rush to dominate the market and outpace any potential competitors, Webvan decided to build a massive, state-of-the-art, automated warehouse. The cost? A whopping $1 billion. This wasn't just any warehouse; it was to be the pinnacle of modern technology and efficiency. Webvan believed that through automation and scale, it could achieve unprecedented delivery times and accuracy.

However, there was a glaring oversight. Webvan's sheer audacity and overconfidence effectively had it putting the cart in front of the horse. It had not yet secured the customer base to justify the size and cost of this warehouse. It built a facility that could handle orders for hundreds of thousands of customers, but it only had a small fraction of that in actual customers.

To visualize the scale of Webvan's miscalculation, imagine preparing a lavish feast meant to feed an entire town only to have a handful of people show up to eat. Trucks were coming in and out of the giant warehouse with just a few bags of groceries, zipping through a cavernous space designed to process exponentially more orders. The oversized facility became a running joke, symbolizing Webvan's overly ambitious and premature scaling efforts.

The result? Webvan burned through its capital at an alarming rate and was unable to sustain its operations. Less than two years after its extravagant warehouse became operational, Webvan declared bankruptcy in 2001. It had reportedly lost over $800 million and was forced to lay off two thousand employees.

This warehouse anecdote underscores the dangers of the "get rich quick" mindset. Webvan was so focused on rapid growth and domination that it lost sight of building a sustainable business from the ground up. It serves as a cautionary tale of the perils of overextending in the entrepreneurial world.

CHAPTER 8

MORNING ROUTINES ARE MAGICAL

"It's been said that the first hour is the rudder of the day. If I'm lazy or haphazard in my actions during the first hour after I wake up, I tend to have a fairly lazy and unfocused day. But if I strive to make that first hour optimally productive, the rest of the day tends to follow suit."

—STEVE PAVLINA, *PERSONAL DEVELOPMENT FOR SMART PEOPLE*

Ninety-eight percent of humanity wakes up and waits for cues from the world to determine their attitude for the day. They wait for their Facebook news feed, their email inbox, or that first phone call of the day to decide whether it's going to be a good day or a bad one.

As an entrepreneur, you must join the 2 percent. Wake up and fix your own positive attitude by using productive morning routines before you're bombarded by any cues from the outside world. By doing this, despite the attitudes of the people you interact with, you are committed to having a positive day.

To succeed on your own terms, you must live on your own terms. Take cues only from yourself and other carefully chosen role models and mentors. Walk away from the 98 percent. Don't hang out where they hang out. Don't talk like they talk. Make the decision to be the most optimistic person in the room.

Part of recognizing your value is treating your brain like a temple, not a garbage pit. It would take over a billion dollars to reproduce your mind. Think about how incredible that is! You own a billion-dollar super computer free and clear! Program it to work for you by using the affirmations we spoke about in the first chapter. Choose which authors and gurus deserve your time and attention. Which ones are you going to tune into, and who will serve you the most?

As a business owner, your most important asset is your attitude. No one can take that away from you. The world can be your greatest friend or greatest adversary depending on the framing of your attitude, and a proper attitude is crucial to your success.

Each day is either full of opportunity or hardship. It is simply how you choose to interpret it, how you choose to filter the events that make up your days. How you choose to react to the circumstances in your life determines your future. The best way to fix a positive mental attitude at the start of each day is by implementing a morning routine.

Morning routines are magical. For a new entrepreneur just starting out, there's nothing I would recommend more for systematically improving your life one day at a time. There is no better way to endure the ups and downs of being in business for yourself than by making sure you conquer your mornings. "Win the morning, win the day."

Here's how most mornings go for me:

- 6:00 a.m.: Wake up, drink a glass of water, make coffee
- 6:15–7:15 a.m.: Write in my journal or book, write one thing I'm grateful for
- 7:15–7:45 a.m.: Read a non-fiction book on business, sales, or entrepreneurship
- 7:45–8:05 a.m.: Meditate
- 8:10–8:20 a.m.: Review to-do list and calendar for the day
- 8:20 a.m.: Wake up family, get breakfast going, ready the kids for school
- 9:00 a.m. Tuesday, Thursday, Sunday: Trail run or swim

Everyone in our company is encouraged to have a daily morning routine, some simple disciplines to stick to each morning. It's a perfect way to get your thoughts going in a positive direction before most of the world has even woken up.

Wake up early. Try to wake up before anyone else in your house, between 5:00 and 6:00 a.m. usually works. Invest one to two hours of quiet solitude into yourself, and start your day without any interruptions.

Seizing this first morning win of not resorting to the snooze button is a major feat in and of itself. It sets the tone for the day and shows you, in a small way, that your mind is going to be in control of your body that day. Not the other way around. It's a little reminder that no matter how you're feeling, your mind is capable of overcoming and taking action anyway. Even if you're feeling a bit lazy or negative, you're up, and you have positive momentum to start your day.

Make sure your phone is silenced or off during this time. Only take phone calls if they are extremely urgent and from your most inner circle. Let your inner circle know this is your time. Be short and to the point with them. They should only be calling you during this time for the most important business or emergencies.

JOIN THE 2 PERCENT BY CREATING A READING HABIT

I can't stress enough the importance of reading as a habit that can change your life and propel your business forward. It will help you gain a leg up on the competition and provide you a steady stream of ideas to help you constantly find new ways to improve.

What makes entrepreneurship so special is the ability to custom tailor the inputs to your mind to produce the outputs you desire. It's about having this blank canvas that is your life and being able to paint onto it your distinct, unique vision.

That's what I mean when I say you should recognize and respect your value. Be deliberate about the inputs into your psyche. Inspire your own creativity by feeding your mind with positive words from books you choose, and reflect on how to incrementally improve your life.

Reject society's addiction to social media and constant news-scrolling, and purposefully clear your mind so you can really think. The increased stress levels brought on by trying to drink from the fire hose of information on our smartphones does not encourage creativity. And creativity is the key to achievement.

As I write these pages, I'm applying a method I learned from the book *The Perfect Day Formula*. For seven years, I only had eight thousand words written in this book, roughly thirty pages. My book was stalled because I was waiting for large chunks of time to appear in my schedule in order to write more material. With two businesses and a wife and kids, unfortunately, those large chunks of time never came.

Craig Ballantyne is the author of The Perfect Day Formula and an expert in how habits shape our lives. He suggests that committing to the simple habit of writing a thousand words first thing every morning can help anyone become a productive writer. Just one thousand words per day, about three pages, on whatever project you are currently working on can transform you from an aspiring writer with a few randomly filled notebook pages to a seasoned author producing a steady stream of material.[27]

I embraced this simple habit, and it allowed me to finally complete this book. In a few short months, I was able to write fifty-two thousand words, 250 pages, through the daily discipline of writing just a little bit every morning no matter what.

Don't get me wrong, this routine was not something I looked forward to at first. It was hard forcing myself out of my warm bed a half hour early, before sunrise, to start thinking and typing. Now, it's something I look forward to each morning. These days, you couldn't force me to sleep in, even on a Sunday, because I'm excited to get to my writing.

PHYSICAL EXERCISE—THE MAGIC ELIXIR FOR THE MIND

Once you've mastered the discipline of reading each day, the next most important morning routine is exercise. I often tell our people, "Nobody here cares if you exercise for your body, but you must exercise to sharpen your mind." Here are some of the benefits of exercise on your mind:

---

27   Craig Ballantyne, "The 21-Day Habit Change Challenge," Medium, May 1, 2017, https://medium.com/the-ascent/the-21-day-habit-change-challenge-d281686a0838.

- Decreased stress
- Decreased social anxiety
- Improved processing of emotions
- Short-term euphoria
- Increased energy, focus, and attention
- Improved memory
- Improved blood circulation
- Decreased brain fog

Every sales call, every negotiation, every meeting through-out your day is a small battle or contest for your mind. The sharpest mind wins. Whoever can communicate their ideas with the most clarity and enthusiasm will succeed. They will make the most sales, they will win more negotiations, and their ideas will be adopted by the company more often.

Looking at this list, can you see why exercise is so important to getting ahead?

Start slow. Start with ten minutes per day. Take a walk around the block. Work yourself up to one hour three days a week. Every day, if possible. Once you start to see the benefits, you won't look back.

Three days a week, every week, I go on a trail run or for a swim at the local fitness center. You can ask my family and business colleagues, I rarely ever miss my exercise. To me, it's as important as a religious practice for my physical and mental health. I would recommend you implement a similar routine.

You'll notice that your ambition to succeed and ability to get things done are contingent on making sure you exercise. Because when you exercise, you're not only working out your body; your brain is also getting the extra blood and oxygen it needs to work at its highest levels. On the rare occasions I skip my exercise, I feel lazy and sluggish. But after a run or a swim, my brain feels sharp again, ready to conquer the world.

GOAL-SETTING MASTERY

What are you working toward that drives you to wake up every morning before everyone else? What keeps you going when it gets tough and everyone else has quit? Part of your morning routine must be reminding yourself of your goals.

The X in the RELAX method of success is to "examine your motivations." How would you define success? For most, it's not the actual owning of the stuff that really matters. It's the feeling you think you'll get when you finally have nice things. It's not owning that second home, it's the feeling of freedom to travel there and share your hard-earned time off with loved ones. It's not the amount of money you have in your bank account, it's the feeling of peace, stability, and the respect earned from your family and friends. The feeling of being someone who can inspire others through your example, someone who can be counted on and looked up to. Keep this in mind if your list of goals is dominated by acquiring material things, which most likely won't give you the long-term satisfaction you're expecting.

More than a decade ago, I invested in a coaching program through Brian Tracy. I ponied up all my savings at the time and waited with anxious anticipation for the coaching package to come in the mail. It came in a beautiful, leather-bound binder that helped me brainstorm ideas for what I really wanted to achieve in life.

The key to the exercise was that you had to completely block out of your mind considerations about whether or not you knew how to get or do the things on your list. And for the purpose of the exercise, *your yearly income has now become your monthly income.*

I was forced to think about the following:

- What do I really want?
- Where do I really want to go?
- What do I really want to do?
- Who do I really want to be?

Forty minutes later, with beads of sweat dripping down my face, I had completed the exercise and came up with a list of 101 goals. The exercise was exciting and powerful and became the foundation for much of my decision-making in the following years.

I encourage you to perform this exercise. It has the potential to give you a laser focus on what you are working for in your day-to-day life, even though some of your goals will likely be years in the future.

Another way to help remind yourself of your goals is by using a vision board.

Vision boards are a great way to motivate yourself in the mornings. A vision board, or a dream board, is a collage of pictures and words of your dreams and desires that serves as a shot of inspiration and motivation every time you look at it. It should contain images of what your ideal life would look like if you had $100 million in the bank and could do whatever you wanted.

Part of the A, "act as if," is reminding yourself that to have the things you want to have in life (a.k.a. the images on your vision board), you must do the things successful people do. And to routinely do the things successful people do, you must embody the habits of a successful person; you must *be* successful. Be–do–have, in that order.

The simple routine of envisioning yourself with future success, having all that you want to have, will trigger the law of attraction and subconsciously direct you to be the person you need to be. This, in turn, will allow you to do whatever it takes to find the opportunities and take the necessary actions to propel yourself along the path of having everything you ever wanted.

I have pictures of my family, surfing and diving in Hawaii and Central America, and the beaches of the world all over my office walls.

I always have a vision board next to the desk in my office. I'm a surfer and a SCUBA diver, and I want my kids to grow up in the ocean. Although we're based in Southern California, my work ethic (and the cold water) doesn't allow us to enjoy our favorite hobbies very often. Many of the photos on my vision board show our family and others enjoying these activities in tropical destinations.

If I continue to hit my goals, I will be able to eventually work less and focus more on my hobbies and passions. These are the things I'll be doing with my future spare time. Each morning, I usually take a minute to stare at my vision board as I sip my coffee. I close my eyes and visualize what my life will be like when I have less responsibilities and more time to enjoy. Then, I can put myself to work, remembering my light at the end of the tunnel.

Keep these things front and center on the walls of your bedroom or your bathroom mirror. Plaster the walls of your office with everything that reminds you of your goals and what motivates you.

When I first realized the importance of goals, I wasn't lucky enough to have my own office. So I took my girlfriend's lipstick and wrote $100,000 on the bathroom mirror. I didn't make

$100,000 that year, but the following year, I earned $111,000, breaking through the six-figure barrier in my mid-twenties. Could I have achieved this without looking at $100,000 written in bright-red lipstick every day for a year? Maybe, but probably not. It became ingrained in my brain, a clear goal I was shooting for. My mind was programmed to look for opportunities that would help me to achieve my goal.

For years, I have used a simple technique of writing savings goal numbers on the calendar by my desk in my home office. Every Friday, I have a number there that is cumulative of what my savings goals are.

During the years I was saving for my beachfront property in Nicaragua, I needed to save $5,000 per week. In the bottom corner of each Friday on the calendar, I wrote 5, 10, 15, and so on up to the total it would take to buy the acre and a half on the beach. When I was able to draw a little checkmark next to the number on my calendar each Friday, it gave me that little boost of gratification from hitting my goal. Drawing that check mark each week gave me the spark of achievement that allowed me to keep going each and every day. This was one of the simple rituals that energized me.

Jerry Seinfeld has said he had a similar practice to give him that same daily boost of achievement. He forced himself to write one joke per day. Every day he wrote a new joke, he made a red X on his calendar for that day. It was this simple act he accomplished each day that kept him going. This simple discipline is how he became Jerry Seinfeld, one of the most successful comedians of our time.

MEDITATION MAKES YOUR BRAIN WORK BETTER

What do Tony Robbins (the greatest motivational speaker of our time), Oprah (the most famous talk show host of our time), Jerry Seinfeld (the most successful comedian of our time), and Ray Dalio (the founder of the largest hedge fund in the world) all have in common?

They are all regular practitioners of meditation.

Do you ever feel like your thoughts are jumbled and disorganized?

Do you feel stressed and like there's too much on your plate?

Do you feel your days go too fast and there's not enough time in the day to get everything done?

I have a prescription for you.

Take a class, read a book, or watch a video on how to meditate. Or start by using a guided meditation on YouTube. Then, practice it every day at least once a day. Go to a quiet place, and give yourself twenty minutes of peace and tranquility. See your thoughts go by on the movie screen of your mind, and let them float away. Learn to quiet your mind until it is thoughtless and calm.

Mario Orsatti, a meditation teacher described in the book *Super Mind*, explains the effects of meditation like this:[28]

> You're going to be more present in your conversations, and in meetings, in one-to-one or in group settings. Your mind's going to be quieter, simpler, and more able to hear what people are saying and why they're saying it... This is really one of the major factors that helps to develop leadership: that quality that when you're communicating with someone, you are really present and listening.

---

28   Norman E. Rosenthal, *Super Mind: How to Boost Performance and Live a Richer and Happier Life through Transcendental Meditation* (New York: Tarcher Perigee, 2016), 180–181.

Meditation slows down your thoughts. It trains your mind to operate at a higher level. It makes you more energized, centered, and purposeful. It helps you become more intentional and less reactive in your words and actions, which, in turn, makes you a better leader and a more effective business owner.

Years ago, the topic of meditation seemed to be coming up more and more in the books I was reading. I noticed most high achievers practiced this discipline, and I decided I needed to find space for it in my daily routine.

I took a course on transcendental meditation seven years ago and started meditating at least once a day. The clarity that it brings to your mind is unbelievable. It allows your conscious mind to settle, which gives you the power to pull ideas and thoughts from your subconscious to your conscious mind. Ray Dalio, in describing meditation, says, "It helps slow things down so that I can act calmly even in the face of chaos, just like a ninja in a street fight."[29]

Some of the benefits reported by regular practitioners of meditation include:

- Improved ability to separate things that matter from irrelevancies
- Increased efficiency in making decisions and taking action
- Help to "work smarter, not just harder" and improved creativity
- Decreased emotional reactivity
- Increased energy leading to a better ability to make healthy choices

---

29   Ray Dalio, *Principles* (New York: Avid Reader Press, 2017), 200.

In my own experience with meditation, I've found my memory has improved and solutions to problems come more easily. Also, situations that used to stress me out no longer have that power. When others on our team are at a stress level of ten because of a problem in our business, I'm calmly sitting at a three or four, thinking two steps ahead about how we're going to resolve it and come out the other end unscathed.

It is said that even during the Cuban Missile Crisis, President John F. Kennedy would take a daily nap in the oval office. It may be what kept us out of a nuclear war.

Meditation is like taking a super-powered nap once or twice a day. Oprah believes in the practice so strongly she shuts down her company for twenty minutes twice a day, at 10:00 a.m. and 4:00 p.m. She knows the productivity lost is negligible compared to the clarity of thought and ninja-like decision-making gained during this time.

As a business leader, you need to operate at the ten-thousand-foot level more often than those who work for you. You must keep an eye on what's most important for the business long term and not get "stuck in the weeds."

My most effective time as the strategic planner for our business is immediately following a meditation session. My thoughts are clear, I have a positive outlook, and I'm calm and relaxed. There is no better time to renew your focus and decide what it is you and your company need to work on next.

As should be evident, morning routines are important to setting your sail for the day. In the next chapter, we'll talk about what follows—how to actually get things done.

CHAPTER 8—ACTION STEPS

- Invest just 1 percent of your earnings into your education. You earn $50,000 a year right now? That's twenty-five books you'll read this year. Watch what that will do to your income next year.
- Try to implement one new thing you learn each day into your life and business.
- Take thirty minutes and brainstorm your goals. Shoot for a list of fifty to one hundred goals. List things you'd like to have or achieve in the next ten years, not just what you think you can get. For the purpose of the exercise, assume your annual income is now your monthly income. What would really do it for you if everything fell into place for you over the next ten years?
- Learn how to meditate. Don't expect it to be easy at first. Give it time. Dedicate at least twenty minutes per day to your meditation practice. Work up to twice a day, forty minutes per day. I promise it's worth it.

INTERLUDE—BLUE BOTTLE COFFEE,
SLOW BURN COMPANY

In 2001, a weary traveling clarinetist named James Freeman decided to leave music behind and go into the coffee business. His vision was to source higher-quality coffee beans and freshly roast them—no more than forty-eight hours old—to provide superior coffee than could be found at Dunkin or Starbucks.

Freeman rented a 186-square-foot potting shed in an alley behind a restaurant and purchased a roaster direct from the manufacturer, driving it from Idaho to California himself. He meticulously roasted seven pounds at a time at no more than five hundred degrees, careful not to over roast the beans like his competitors. Blue Bottle Coffee was born.

Blue Bottle gained a cult following in the Oakland and San Francisco area, selling pounds of freshly roasted beans and cups of coffee direct to consumers at farmers' markets.

As it grew into brick-and-mortar locations, secret off-menu items strengthened the brand and mystique of the company. Drinks like the "Gibraltar," a strong mini latte served in a glass tumbler, and treats like the "Wafelgato," a Belgian waffle with a scoop of ice cream and their house espresso dripped over top, attracted increasingly larger crowds to its stores.

Freeman admits due to his lack of business acumen at the time, he purposefully had to grow cautiously and not let his ambition get the best of him. He was quoted as saying he always made sure to end each month with "money left in the bank account."[30]

Blue Bottle grew in popularity because of its dedication to artisanal coffee and slow-brew methods, with its baristas famously stepping up onto stools to pour hot water, a little at a time, over freshly ground beans.

In 2012, Blue Bottle Coffee was a well-regarded but still relatively small coffee roastery and cafe with a devout following in the Bay Area. Around this time, the company received a substantial investment offer from a venture capital firm that could have significantly accelerated its expansion.

However, James Freeman and the leadership team chose a different path. They decided to decline the investment despite its promise of rapid growth and potential quick returns. Instead, they remained dedicated to their principles of sourcing high-quality beans, meticulously roasting them, and serving the best possible coffee, even if it meant growing at a more measured pace.

They exemplified the "slow burn" approach in the competitive coffee industry.

Blue Bottle Coffee's leaders recognized that taking the venture capital investment would likely lead to compromises on their core values. It could result in faster expansion but potentially

---

30   Tom Huddleston Jr. and Beatriz Bajuelos, "Blue Bottle Coffee: How a Struggling Clarinet Player Used $15,000 in Credit Card Debt to Launch a $700 Million Brand," CNBC, July 12, 2019, https://www.cnbc.com/2019/07/12/blue-bottle-coffee-went-from-single-coffee-cart-to-700-million-brand.html.

at the cost of the distinct experience that defined their brand. They understood that maintaining their commitment to the unique cafe experience was vital for their long-term success.

As a result of this decision, Blue Bottle Coffee continued to expand gradually and deliberately, with an unwavering dedication to the craft of coffee. The company steadily opened new locations, maintained close relationships with coffee producers, and invested in quality-control measures.

Over time, this "slow burn" approach paid off. Blue Bottle Coffee's reputation for excellence in coffee craftsmanship became more widely recognized. In 2015, the company secured additional investment from alternative sources, allowing it to expand without compromising its values. Eventually, in 2017, Nestlé acquired a majority stake in Blue Bottle Coffee for nearly $500 million, a testament to the brand's unique position in the coffee market.

Even in a fast-paced industry like coffee, a commitment to maintaining core values, quality, and a unique experience rather than succumbing to a "get rich quick" mentality that might compromise a brand's integrity and authenticity can lead to long-term success. Blue Bottle Coffee's dedication to the art of coffee brewing and its "slow burn" philosophy contributed to its rise as a respected and enduring player in the coffee world.

CHAPTER 9

GETTING THINGS DONE

"It does not take much strength to do things, but it requires a great deal of strength to decide what to do."

—ELBERT HUBBARD

When I first got into business for myself almost a decade ago, I got together with my business partner at the time, and we made plans for years into the future. We planned to expand our solar business into different markets, add a telemarketing division, and diversify into debt collection and other assorted industries.

We spent our money on new ideas and distractions as fast as it came in. We had extravagant company bonus vacations planned for our sales team. And we insisted on having a twelve-foot-by-forty-foot poster listing bonuses in full color covering one of our office walls.

I had a thousand things on my mental to-do list every day and constantly felt like I had to run in ten different directions at one hundred miles per hour to be "successful." Looking back, I probably drove everyone crazy.

Many new entrepreneurs fall into the trap of forcing upon

themselves an artificial timeline to achieve "overnight success." Maybe you're twenty-four years old, and you say to yourself, "I must retire by thirty, and to do so, I'm going to build my business to $15 million and have twenty rental properties in my portfolio and a net worth of $10 million dollars." Now don't get me wrong, that's a great goal and an admirable timeline. But is it worth slaving away in a never-ending grind during some of the best years of your life?

The RELAX method tells you to slow down. "Slow is smooth, smooth is fast." Who are you becoming and what are you learning along the way? That's the real value. Be careful not to rob yourself of the fulfillment that comes from being a successful person and having the ability to pull up others around you. Soak in the wisdom you're gaining that you'll be able to impart on your employees and the younger generation someday.

Learning how to focus and take one thing at a time is the first step. In the beginning, we were the definition of a business with a lack of focus. Yes, our main business was solar panels, but we were already way beyond that, planning into the future for when we would be swimming in money. Instead of focusing on today, we were focused two to three years into the future, and we barely had a business yet. We were both chasing squirrels for an entire year. Although we sold $1.8 million in solar systems our first year, my business partner experienced stress-induced shock and left California to go back home to Tennessee.

Yes, it's important to "act as if" your habits and attitudes are those of someone more successful than you. But it's important to maintain the discipline of staying grounded and be realistic about your current situation so you don't prematurely burn through your resources—your energy and your cash.

After our year of frantic squirrel chasing, I brought in my little brother Matt to partner with me and help me renew my focus by learning to prioritize. After years in academia at University of Cincinnati and Penn State University, Matt had a methodical way of creating a to-do list and sticking to it throughout the day. Fortunately, this rubbed off on me and had a huge effect on my future. Instead of trying to take on the world every day, we just took on one single notebook page of tasks. Each and every day, we slowed down, talked about what we needed to do, wrote it down, and then executed.

I didn't realize it at the time, but looking back now, I was in the midst of making the discoveries that led to this book, learning the power of the RELAX method to success. And the proof was in the pudding: despite feeling less ambitious and working much more slowly and deliberately, we doubled our numbers the second year and hit $3.6 million in top-line sales. I'm a huge fan of thinking big, but we learned together to take it one quarter—three months—at a time. Take that quarter and break it down into weeks then into days. Then decide, "If I only had today, what would I need to do?"

What are the six most important things you need to do today? Write them all down in a leather-bound business notebook. Now think, *What is the top priority? What is the second-highest priority?* Number them one to six to make sure it's clear in your brain what needs to be worked on and in what order. Do this every day.

Echoing the words of Gary W. Keller in his book *The One Thing*, "Today what's the one thing I can do for my one thing, such that by doing it everything else will be easier or unnecessary?"[31] That should be number one on your list. That's worth repeating, "*Today what's the one thing I can do for my one thing,*

---

31   Gary W. Keller, *The ONE Thing: The Surprisingly Simple Truth about Extraordinary Results* (Portland, OR: Bard Press, 2013), p7.

such that by doing it everything else will be easier or unneces-sary?" Work on that task today until it is complete. It doesn't matter if you get to number two. It will be there tomorrow. If you get distracted by a phone call or an urgent piece of mail from the licensing department or the tax board, make sure you get back to your number-one task. What this does is it forces you to get the most mission-critical, valuable tasks done first. If you only complete three out of your six most-important tasks for the day, that's okay. At least you were working on the most important and got them done.

If you complete all six mission-critical tasks and it's 6:00 p.m. instead of 8:00 p.m., reward yourself. Don't start on the rest of your list. Go home and see your family early. Grab a beer with a friend. Do something that will reward your accomplishment and have you salivating to have a productive day tomorrow, like one of Pavlov's dogs.

A couple years ago, we had a very highly paid and talented consultant, the previously mentioned Coach Brian. Brian always brought us back to, "Guys, what's going to *move the needle*?" In other words, is the thing you're working on going to be important for the growth of the company? For you to hit your goals and continue the growth trend you're tracking on? Or are you doing busywork? Majoring in minor things? Are you working on things that will not *move the needle*?

THINKING AND PLANNING

Thinking, yes, actually sitting down and taking the time to think, is the hardest task for most people to do, and that's why most people never engage in it. In our age of social media and instant gratification, of constant phone scrolling, it is easier to consume information than actually "put your thinking cap on" and think for yourself. But it is the most valuable and highly rewarded activity a human being can do. George Bernard Shaw once said, "Few people think more than two or three times a year. I have made an international reputation for myself by thinking once or twice a week."[32]

The masses want others to think and plan their lives for them. This is an effect of our school system being designed to produce employees or followers. But those who can think for themselves and solve problems on a regular basis become the leaders, the successful entrepreneurs and business owners in our society. According to Earl Nightingale, founder of Nightingale-Conant and pioneer of audiobook learning, there is a very simple method to solving your problems and having a successful life: pull out a notebook in the morning, write your number-one goal or problem at the top of the page, and start to write solutions or better ways to do what you're doing.[33] Take as long as you need to come up with twenty solutions or new ideas every day.

This goes back to the R and the E. "Recognize your value," "exercise your creativity," and discipline yourself to only work on the highest-value activities. Work smart, not hard. One of the most profitable habits you can practice is to use your time to reflect on ways to grow your business. Brainstorm how to produce more with the resources you have on hand at any given moment. Exercise and unleash your creativity by developing the habits that will program your mind and empower you to be a better leader. You'll become the person that others call on for ideas and solutions.

---

32   "I Have Made an International Reputation for Myself by Thinking Once or Twice a Week," Quote Investigator, February 20, 2014, https://quoteinvestigator.com/2014/02/20/shaw-think/.

33   Earl Nightingale, "The Great Problem-Solving Tool," Nightingale-Conant, accessed April 22, 2024, https://www.nightingale.com/articles/the-great-problem-solving-tool/.

Similar to idea mining with voice recorders, the twenty-solutions method has a profound compounding effect. If you do this five days a week, that's five thousand new ideas over the course of a year. Of course, they're not all going to be winners. But do you think one in one thousand might be a million-dollar idea? Absolutely.

As an entrepreneur and leader of an organization, it's extremely important to always plan your days ahead of time. Ideally, the night before. Have your days planned out before they start. Once your company has more than a handful of people in it, you will likely be bombarded with managerial tasks throughout your day. Phone calls asking how to solve higher-level problems with disgruntled customers. People sending you documents that only you can authorize. Your business partner calling to ask what color sweaters you should give away at the Christmas party.

You must decide each night what you are trying to accomplish tomorrow. What is your most important, highest-priority activity? Ask yourself questions like, "What is the most profitable activity I can work on tomorrow?"

In our solar and roofing business, priorities usually ebb and flow between recruiting, pushing the sales, and supporting collections. We go through periods where our sales will dip, and the focus becomes recruiting fresh blood or pushing our current team to sell more. Whether it's goal setting or motivational training, we have to light a fire to encourage our salespeople to go out there and "get theirs" that day and bring in more customers. Once we're heavy on sales, we'll make a push to ensure the money gets collected. When our sales and cash flow are taken care of, I can actually work on the business versus in the business. I can turn my focus to our company strategy and improving the processes that move the company toward growth.

LAST WEEK IS GONE

It is important to clean your slate at the beginning of each week. I like to do this on Sunday nights. Are my priorities this week the same as last week, or do I need to reassess? What are on my recorders from last week's reflections that I need to focus on this week?

Each Sunday night, create a to-do list in your leather-bound business notebook for the coming week and break it down by day. Look back onto last week's to-do lists and see if any mission-critical tasks were missed. Put these on your Monday list. This is why it's important to have your to-dos in a leather-bound notebook, not on scraps of paper or the backs of envelopes that will eventually get shoved into an office drawer somewhere or thrown into the trash.

I have saved eight years of my notebooks, and it's always fun to look back, years into the past, and see what I was working on. It's a good way to get perspective and realize how far you've come, how much more effective of a person and business owner you have become.

Asana is also a great tool I've been using for the past few years. It's an efficient way to organize your goals, projects, and tasks. Often, I'll refer to Asana two to three times per week to check in and make sure I'm not forgetting to do anything for my company or personal to-dos that got missed.

DON'T WORRY ABOUT DOING EVERYTHING

As a new entrepreneur, you will tend to try to do everything and be there for everyone all the time. To answer all the questions and solve all the problems that pass through the giant bottleneck in your company, which is typically you. Most people in your new company will expect this from you, their leader. Not only is this stressful and unsustainable, it is very unproductive.

You need to decide when during your day is your "maker time" (working on the business) and when is your "manager time" (working in the business).

Your manager time is divided up into smaller time slots, usually fifteen minutes to an hour, and dominated by meetings, phone calls, and emails. When you're in manager mode, you spend a lot of time being reactive, putting out fires and dealing with so-called "emergencies." More or less making sure the trains run on time. It is impossible for you to be in manager mode all day and get anything productive done.

This is why most companies plateau: their owners, in the beginning, have plenty of creative, productive time. They are acting as makers, working on the business. After all, this is how the company gets off the ground, with marketing, sales, and creation of something that a short time ago did not exist. This is the magic of entrepreneurs—we can create something from nothing.

Once the young company has grown to a point where the lower-value activities need to be delegated, your creative time gets limited by managerial time. There is no question things like administrative work, data entry, and communication with suppliers must be turned over to your staff. However, for each person you add to your company, it nearly triples the amount of communication and complication.

Your lower-paid employees will likely not understand productivity and time management and oftentimes want to have all of their problems solved by you, their boss. You must remove the bottleneck as soon as possible and empower your employees to start thinking for themselves. It is helpful to create a rule like, "Try three ways to figure out any problem before bringing it to management."

Commit to deciding on, blocking off, and regaining control

of your maker time. Maker time is typically larger increments of time, usually one- to four-hour blocks. Maker time is when you are producing, creating. It is your most important time, and you must protect it. For a growing company, maker time is recruiting and thinking of new ads to hire sharp new talent. It is prospecting, selling, and finding new customers, often while training a sales team to do the same.

During this time, you can type out new sales scripts or create sales training. You can design customer-satisfaction surveys and employee-training programs. You can research online trade magazines and supplier publications to answer the questions, "What is the new direction for my industry? What is likely to change in the next couple years?"

This is the time when you need to be left alone to think clearly, create, and strategize.

I try to get in at least two two-hour blocks of maker time per day. One in the morning from 6:00 a.m. to 8:00 a.m. and one in the evening between 5:00 p.m. and 7:30 p.m. During the morning hours, I follow the schedule I detailed earlier, with a focus on "maker" activities, thinking, and planning.

You will notice that none of my maker time is during the typical 9:00 a.m. to 5:00 p.m. hours, when everyone else is in the office or working. What I have found is it is impossible to get "real work" done in the office when you have other people there demanding your time and attention.

This is your manager time, and some may say a lot of this time is unnecessary. I would say, for productivity, yes, this time is 80 percent unnecessary. But for camaraderie and cultivating relationships with the people who make up your team, arguably, this time is important. Although, absolutely, periods of time at the office are spent in frivolous conversation and "grab-ass" that could be eliminated to create a more efficient, but less fun, company. For example, I have had a ping-pong table in most of my offices, and you couldn't pay me to remove it!

EVERYTHING IS NOT AN EMERGENCY

Me: Oscar, you missed my phone call. I can't have you missing my phone calls. What if we miss a call from a major customer and we lose them because you didn't have your phone with you?

Oscar: Does it really matter that much? I called you back ten minutes later.

Me: Absolutely, it all matters. Keep your phone with you at all times. All the successful people I know are available all the time.

This was my attitude eight years ago. I worked twelve- to sixteen-hour days and ate every meal out. I chugged down two twenty-ounce Red Bulls every day to keep my energy and intensity up. I neglected my health in the name of being in constant contact with everyone in my business. As a result, I gained fifty pounds and started having frequent heart palpitations and even chest pains.

I was on the phone and available from 7:00 a.m. to 11:00 p.m., sometimes later. Whenever I didn't feel busy, I would get one of my sales people on the horn to check on them and make sure everyone was producing. I made sure every customer had my phone number and was on call 24/7 to ensure I never lost one.

Like a surgeon, I imagined every situation was a 9-1-1, life-or-death emergency, and I frantically put out fires. I was micromanaging our sales team and our solar and roofing crews.

With our marketing team, I was out canvassing, knocking on doors with them three days a week. The other three days, I was in houses until 10:00 p.m. or 11:00 p.m., shadowing our sales people far past their "learning curve," months after they were trained. I wanted to make sure they were saying everything exactly as I trained them to keep our closing percentages high.

As for our crews, I would often show up before them at job sites around 6:30 a.m., just to make sure they arrived on time. And then I'd collect all their personal cell phone numbers so if they didn't arrive punctually the next time, they'd get an earful.

I was a maniac.

I was on my way to my first major burnout in business. My methods were unsustainable, and I knew it. But I continued with them out of greed and fear. I was making $30,000 to $50,000 per month during this time, but I was constantly juggling ten plates in the air at once.

I was afraid to let go and stop juggling out of fear of losing my whole business or having it all come crashing down. I started having chest pains and anxiety attacks. I would drink glass after glass of scotch whisky (yes, scotch, I thought I was Ron Burgundy) at the office each night to calm down while continuing to work, often late into the night.

At the end of two years of this jaded philosophy, I threw my hands up, gave 85 percent of my business to my brother and my general manager, and left to go to Nicaragua and Florida for seven months. Four months in, my general manager had swiped my entire company and started his own business, using everything I had taught him. My brother had left California and gone back to Pennsylvania to seek the comfort of his girlfriend.

I came back to California eight months later, tail between my legs, and was forced to start from scratch. This time, I was going to recruit faster, work more, and push people even harder. No, the lesson had not been learned. I partnered with my good friend Oscar, my best sales person from 2016, whom I was chastising at the beginning of this section for not answering his phone.

Two years later, we had built two offices, were back up to $6 million in annual top-line sales, and had a team of thirty-five people. We had a weak foundation built on both of us being workaholics and micromanaging every aspect of our business.

Our nerves frayed and emotions sensitive, we ended up having several big fights and lost half our staff. Oscar and I decided to part ways, despite having the best year—in terms of the numbers—either of us had ever had.

This time, I recognized I had a problem and needed to make some changes. I learned to meditate and committed to practicing meditation a minimum of once a day, usually twice a day. I learned everything was not an emergency. Magically, during a twenty-minute meditation, things would work themselves out. I would call back the people whose calls I had missed, and they'd say, "I called you, but I can't remember what I was calling about." Or even better, "Yeah, I needed you for x, y, or z, but I figured it out."

I discovered I could have balance in my life and own a business at the same time. I adopted a "live and let live" philosophy. I came to terms with the fact that most people I hired would never have the ambition and drive I do, and I would often push them away with my extreme intensity. Like Tina Fey in the movie *Mean Girls*, I realized, "I am a pusher, I push people."

It might be that I push myself because I do love helping people. In fact, part of our documented company purpose is to embody a "Robinhood mentality—helping our middle-class customers get what they're entitled to from deep-pocketed insurance companies." And with solar, allowing our customers to "take control and have energy independence from greedy fossil-fuel electric companies."

I also feel a great deal of satisfaction seeing our employees succeed, provide for their families, and develop as human beings. One of my greatest sources of fulfillment at my job is watching someone grow—in confidence and ability—to levels they never thought possible.

But I implemented a new ultimatum: if I needed to sacrifice my health for my business, it wasn't worth it. My health became the priority. To this day, as already noted, I meditate daily and run or swim three days per week, religiously. We call them "clarity breaks," and everyone in our leadership team has an assigned clarity break at least once a week.

I committed to being home in the mornings and working from my home office to be with my kids for breakfast. I made my schedule less strenuous and made sure I was getting home by around 7:30 p.m. so I could spend some time with them before they went to bed.

Life as an entrepreneur doesn't need to be a frantic fire drill. Your ability to systematically reduce your business's reliance on you, the owner, will have a direct effect on your freedom and overall happiness. We aggressively implemented processes in our business, and each member of our leadership team is assigned to document a new process every quarter. Slowly but surely, our staff began to rely on the systems we put in place as opposed to constantly depending on me and the other members of the leadership team.

You'll begin to see that the world carries on without your direct involvement in it. Your sanity as the business owner is paramount. The employees and contractors in your company depend on you for their livelihoods. Your mental and physical health is your most valuable asset, and you must protect it.

After all, what if you get rich and then die of a heart attack before you can enjoy the freedom with your family?

In the next chapter, we'll look at a life hack that will help you build up your savings and allow you to take advantage of the financial opportunities that routinely present themselves.

CHAPTER 9—ACTION STEPS

- Throughout the day, ask yourself, "If I get only one thing done today, will I be happy with what I'm working on right now?"
- Never start your day without making a one-page list of to-dos, numbered one to six. Start working on number one first then move on to number two and so on.
- Get the productivity tool Asana. It's free until you have more than five users.
- Block off and designate your maker time. Protect this time every day, barring unforeseen "emergencies" where someone needs your attention. Decide on a sustainable routine that you can keep up assuming your business will last ten years into the future.
- Decide on a clarity break at least once a week. Usually these are best if you can get outside and into nature. Go for a run in the woods a couple days a week. Take a bike ride around a lake. Do a sunrise hike before you come to work. Get in a photography session at sunset once a week.

INTERLUDE—THERANOS, *GET RICH QUICK* COMPANY

Theranos was a health-technology startup founded by Elizabeth Holmes in 2003 and was hyped as a groundbreaking company poised to transform the medical industry.

Holmes, a Stanford dropout, founded Theranos with a grand vision: to make medical testing more convenient and affordable. She claimed to have developed a technology that could run a wide range of tests using just a few drops of blood.

Theranos secured substantial funding and attention due to its innovative claims. Holmes's unwavering confidence played a significant role in attracting investors and influential board members.

Theranos partnered with pharmacy behemoth Walgreens to offer its blood test kits in their stores, promising quicker results at lower costs than traditional tests. High-profile partnerships elevated Theranos's reputation and created anticipation for the company's potential to disrupt the healthcare industry.

The company's infamous blood-testing machine had been named "Edison." Holmes often touted the machine's amazing ability to run comprehensive tests using just a few drops of blood. In reality, the device was notoriously unreliable and routinely malfunctioned.

When representatives from Walgreens visited Theranos's headquarters in Palo Alto to see a demo of its amazing machines before partnering with Theranos, the stakes were high. As the visitors were shown the machine in action, it suddenly stopped working. Rather than admit to the technical glitch, Theranos employees secretly ran the tests on traditional machines while telling the Walgreens team that the Edison was doing the work. It was a desperate game of make-believe, worthy of a heist movie.

The Theranos team went to elaborate lengths to keep up the facade. Employees were under strict orders not to disclose Edison's limitations, and many worked in silos, not fully grasping the extent to which the technology was flawed. Holmes maintained a culture of secrecy within the company, limiting access to information and preventing transparency about the technology's shortcomings.

Eventually, investigations by The Wall Street Journal and others uncovered the serious issues within Theranos. The company had clearly misled investors, partners, and patients about the capabilities of its technology.

The US Food and Drug Administration and the Centers for Medicare & Medicaid Services (CMS) raised concerns about Theranos's practices, leading to sanctions and a revocation of the company's lab certifications.

In 2016, the US Securities and Exchange Commission (SEC) began investigating Holmes and former Theranos President Ramesh "Sunny" Balwani and eventually charged them with several counts of fraud. In September 2018, Theranos was officially dissolved, and its remaining assets were distributed to creditors.

The company's rapid rise, once valued at $10 billion, had come to a spectacular and stunning end. Holmes was sentenced in November 2022 to eleven years and three months in federal prison for defrauding investors of hundreds of millions of dollars.

The Walgreens episode and the whole story of Theranos capture the company's audacity and its commitment to appearance over substance. Holmes and her team went to extreme lengths to project an image of success rather than admit faults and take the "slow burn" approach of actually developing the cutting-edge technology they aspired to create.

CHAPTER 10

STAY BROKE TO STAY HUNGRY

"Stay broke. I said broke—not poor. I have a policy to never, ever have money sitting around. Once I started increasing income, I immediately moved the surpluses to sacred accounts that were out of my reach and marked for future investments."

—GRANT CARDONE

According to a recent LendingClub survey reported by CNBC, 62 percent of Americans are living paycheck to paycheck.[34] Inflation and a high cost of living are being blamed for putting the majority of the population in a situation where they have no room to breathe financially. Back to the RELAX mentality, you must "recognize your value" and reject going through life red-lining your bank account. Make a vow to yourself that you won't be caught in that trap.

---

34   Jessica Dickler, "62% of Americans Are Still Living Paycheck to Paycheck, Making It 'The Main Financial Lifestyle,' Report Finds," CNBC, October 31, 2023, https://www.cnbc.com/2023/10/31/62percent-of-americans-still-live-paycheck-to-paycheck-amid-inflation.html.

If you're serious about making it as an entrepreneur, you'll have to "leap out of your comfort zone" and not spend your money like the rest of the American middle class. Temporarily make some lifestyle sacrifices to build up your war chest of savings in order to survive the inevitable valleys of business ownership. Create a discipline to save first then pay bills then spend, in that order. Refuse to live like those with their heads barely above water.

Admittedly, I was terrible at saving money in my twenties, so in my thirties, I implemented some hacks that have helped a great deal. Based on a recommendation from Grant Cardone, the first thing I've done is establish a policy to never keep more than $2,000 in my personal checking account. Grant built a real estate empire by tricking himself into thinking he was broke. This way, not only was he able to build up his savings to make significant real estate investments, he also never lost his hustle.

If you were *fortunate* enough to have had some struggle in your life, think back to the times when you only had a few hundred dollars to your name. You had to figure out how to survive, pay your bills, and put food on the table for yourself and your family.

How resourceful were you?

Did you fill your refrigerator and your pantry with $1,000 of groceries from Costco or did you settle for $100 of the necessary items from Aldi that could get you through the week?

Did you go to a restaurant and eat out, spending $100 at lunch or $200 on a nice dinner, or pack your lunch and cook ramen noodles or macaroni and cheese at home? I'll confess, I unashamedly devoured plenty of gourmet plates of ramen noodles and grilled cheese "a la cart" in college and for years after.

How about at your work?

Did you go through your day very laissez-faire and have the

attitude of "Whatever gets done today is okay with me"? No. Most likely you had a pep in your step, making sure to hustle and get done as much as you possibly could.

You made that call to that intimidating prospect you'd been putting off for a week. You tracked down that money one of your biggest customers owed you for a month. You made moves.

What if you were able to operate with this sense of urgency for your whole career? Or at least ten years of it? You'd make things happen, probably even become a millionaire.

I've seen the hustle muscle wear out time and time again with ex-business partners and sales reps. It's a very common downfall. Once most people have a few thousand dollars to their name, they feel very comfortable and don't have any urgency to work hard or make more sales that month or even that year.

Don't be that person. Get that money out of your checking account. Put it somewhere you can't see it, like in a safety deposit box or an obscure credit union savings account where they make it hard for you to withdraw.

The RELAX method doesn't rely on willpower alone. Humans only have a finite amount of willpower. Most have good intentions to save, good intentions to curb their poor spending habits, but the majority rely on sheer willpower to hold themselves accountable day to day.

In his book *Atomic Habits*, James Clear highlights the importance of a "commitment device" to make your bad habits more difficult. He says, "Commitment devices are useful because they enable you to take advantage of good intentions before you can fall victim to temptation."[35]

Imagine this: you are visiting your aging parents in Florida,

---

35   James Clear, *Atomic Habits: An Easy and Proven Way to Build Good Habits and Break Bad Ones* (New York: Avery, 2018), 170.

the land of water toys. All around you, people have nice boats, personal watercrafts, and smiles on their faces. A strong urge overcomes your ego. You are compelled to buy a Sea-Doo jet ski.

Unfortunately, you don't have $12,000 in your checking account to make the purchase, and you definitely don't want to use your precious credit. You'd be forced to drive to a bank, wait in line, sign a paper with a teller, and then get escorted into the back of the bank to get into your safety deposit box. Then you'd have to pull out your own sweat-and-blood-earned, cold, hard cash. How much less likely are you to buy that jet ski?

It simply is too much of a hassle to go retrieve that extra money to spend it on an impulse purchase.

If you're like most people, you're not going to be able to save $100,000 over the course of a couple weeks to make a large investment. You'll need to plan out your savings to hit your goals over the course of two to five years. Set your savings goal at whatever is possible for you, but definitely set *a* goal. Whether it's $200 per week, $1,000 per week, or $5,000 per week, set a goal and take that money out of your checking account and move it somewhere that's hard to access.

When I was purchasing my real estate in Nicaragua, I would wire quantities of $9,500 at a time down to my bank account in Nicaragua. (Amounts over $10,000 raise red flags for money laundering with the US government, so that's a no-no.) In this way, over time, I was able to purchase my first 12.5 acres with a large amount of cash and my 1.5 acres on the beach for even more cash, no debt. The point is as soon as the money had left the US, it was no longer accessible to me for frivolous spending. It was essentially in an ear-marked savings account being readied to make significant real estate investments.

The reason so many Americans are up to their eyeballs in credit card debt is because credit cards are so easy to swipe and forget. Then you send your debt on a magic-carpet ride until you feel like paying off the balance, months or years in the future.

You must fight your own human tendencies. Make it hard to spend your hard-earned money. Make it hurt.

DON'T BE A $30,000 MILLIONAIRE

Following the advice in this book, I have no doubt you will eventually make great money. However, a lot of my colleagues have a common affliction: they start talking a big game and living an even bigger one the moment they have a taste of success.

One friend financed an $80,000 Audi and bought a golf cart after his first great year. Another bought four Razors, to the tune of $100,000, to ride with his family a couple days a year. Acting as if you are a millionaire when you've "arrived" at $30,000 in the bank is a common attitude, but it will not sustain you very long.

Most will go for the toys and lifestyle before they have any sort of nest egg or major investments. This goes back to the previous section about getting that money out of your checking account; otherwise, it will burn a hole in your pocket.

I get it. Most budding entrepreneurs, including me, lived hand-to-mouth for years before they reached some degree of comfort. So, it's nice to reward yourself every now and then for your hard work. But the ego is a very strong force. Your ego wants to show off your newfound wealth to neighbors and friends. But please don't go finance that $80,000 truck or buy that $100,000 RV until you've invested in some real estate.

You won't need that $50,000 boat because you haven't made it yet. You won't even have enough time to use it. Rent the boat for $500 a day for the two days a year you're going to use it and save your money.

The next downturn in your business or the economy is just around the corner, and it's more important to stay in the game than to have a boat. That new RV that has you thinking you've made it will only create complacency and laziness. I promise you the first time you make a big ego-driven purchase before you've actually earned it is when life will inevitably slap you in the face and punish you for being so cocky and naive.

HIDE MONEY FROM YOUR SPOUSE

I have a phrase, a "*dicho*," for my wife: "*Yo digo no hay dinero, y por eso, siempre hay.*" "There's no money, and for that reason, there's always money."

This doesn't go for everybody, but some entrepreneurs I know could benefit enormously from curbing the spending of their spouses.

You are working your ass off toward a dream, and perhaps your spouse doesn't share your struggle, mentally and emotionally. They don't understand the highs and lows. If you make $10,000 in a week, they expect you to make $10,000 every week. And they adjust their lifestyle accordingly.

My wife's biggest vices are shoes, bags, and eating out, often treating her friends and family. Sort of "flashing it around" a bit. And she's a saint compared to some of my friends' spouses, who seem to be on a mission to send their partners into bankruptcy.

I've developed a simple budgeting system. Pick a number, whatever you're comfortable with—I usually stick to either $75,000 to $100,000 per year or $1,500 to $2,000 per week—and live on that amount of money. If you're single, discipline yourself to live on $40,000 per year if you can. Have a discussion with your spouse, "That's the money we must live on." Then, when you earn $200,000 or $400,000 dollars in a year, you have a massive margin for savings and investments. And paying taxes.

It's amazing how difficult this practice is when you start because most salespeople are loose and free with their spending. They have a commission mentality.

"That new $3,000 computer is just one sale. I can go out and make another sale."

"That $10,000 vacation? Simple: three more sales, easy."

But if you can discipline yourself and your family to live well below your means for a few years, you will eventually be rewarded with the financial independence and freedom you deserve.

This is exactly what I mean about trusting the inputs, knowing the results will come, and embracing the mentality of the Slow Burn Entrepreneur. The Slow Burn Entrepreneur goes against the mainstream and knows they don't need to display their success to the world in order to be a success. Because what they have inside is a quiet knowing and the ingrained habits that will bring them success year after year without fail.

Now that you've mastered your money habits, it will be important to learn another tool that helps prevent burn out. I'll tell you what that is in the next chapter.

CHAPTER 10—ACTION STEPS

- Ask yourself, "Could I benefit from some of these extreme measures when it comes to my relationship to money?"
- Find a place to hide money from yourself. That can be a safety deposit box at a big bank, a savings account at an obscure credit union, or simply by pulling out cashier's checks to save money.

- Save first then pay bills then spend what's left—not the other way around, as the middle class does.
- Set a weekly savings goal. Be ambitious—try for 30 percent to 50 percent of your take-home pay. You will thank yourself later.
- Learn to find joy in accumulating savings, not in buying toys you'll use a few days per year.

INTERLUDE—SPANX, *SLOW BURN* COMPANY

Sara Blakely worked a variety of odd jobs in her twenties. She played a chipmunk at Walt Disney World after they told her she was too short to be Goofy. She also tried her hand as a stand-up comedian before landing a job at Danka, an office supply company.

During her years of selling fax machines door to door in the late 1990s, Blakely was frustrated by the discomfort and visibility of pantyhose when she wore open-toed shoes, though she did appreciate the smooth look the pantyhoses' control tops provided. She observed that traditional hosiery didn't provide the versatility she desired.

An idea began to form in Blakely's mind. She envisioned creating shapewear that would provide a smoother and more comfortable alternative to traditional undergarments.

Blakely's breakthrough came when she decided to cut the feet off a pair of pantyhose. Her first thought was, "There's no way someone else hasn't thought of this." But she persisted.

Using $5,000 in savings, Blakely started working on her concept, researching different materials and designs and creating a prototype of her innovative shapewear.

In 2000, Blakely officially launched Spanx with her flagship product: the footless pantyhose. Initially, she sold her invention directly to consumers and relied on word-of-mouth marketing.

Upon fine-tuning her product, Blakely fearlessly cold-called Neiman Marcus and convinced a buyer to allow her to showcase her creation. She modeled the shapewear herself by trying it on in the bathroom, demonstrating its transformative qualities. The buyer was persuaded, and Spanx soon landed on the shelves of select Neiman Marcus stores.

Here's where the "slow burn" value shines through: even as Spanx began to gain traction, Blakely resisted the temptation of external investment. She was extremely wary of relinquishing control too quickly. She feared venture capitalists might not understand her vision or would pressure her into rapid expansion before the brand was ready. And she knew she wanted to own 100 percent of the company.

Instead of seeking venture capital and rapid growth, she prioritized organic growth, focusing on product quality, authenticity, and grassroots marketing. Women quickly embraced the comfort and slimming effects of Spanx, and the product gained a loyal following.

As it grew, Spanx became known for its clever advertising campaigns that helped set the brand apart. One of the most iconic ads it launched was the "We've Got Your Butt Covered" campaign. This tagline instantly conveyed the brand's mission while adding a funny twist, even gaining support from comedian Sarah Silverman and celebrities like Jenny McCarthy.

One of Blakely's pivotal moments came unexpectedly. Oprah Winfrey named Spanx one of her "Favorite Things" in 2000, which launched the brand to national recognition. Yet, even with the surge in attention and potential business deals knocking down her door, Blakely remained true to her steady approach. She took her time to grow Spanx thoughtfully and sustainably.

Without ever taking any outside investment, she went on to turn Spanx into a global powerhouse that has changed the lives of women all over the world. Blakely has been named one of *Time* magazine's 100 Most Influential People in the World and was featured on the cover of *Forbes* magazine as the youngest self-made female billionaire.

Through her personal foundation, Blakely has given millions of dollars to help elevate other women, and in 2013, she signed the Giving Pledge, promising to donate half her wealth to philanthropy. Blakely's dedication to her initial vision and her "slow burn" strategy is a significant reason for her success.

CHAPTER 11

GIVE YOURSELF A BREAK

"The enemy of all champions is physical and emotional burnout, and they will go to great lengths in the performance planning process to ensure burnout never occurs more than once."

—STEVE SIEBOLD, *177 MENTAL TOUGHNESS SECRETS OF THE WORLD CLASS*

I was having the best year of my life in 2016. Solar was in its second year of a boom phase, and electricity prices were soaring. Everyone was jumping on the renewable-energy bandwagon, and my solar business in Southern California was reaping the rewards.

I was constantly trying to keep up with our GM, who was hiring five new canvassers per week to hunt for us, marketing solar, while I was hiring and training seasoned salespeople to go in and close the sales. Most weeks, I was taking home paychecks of $10,000 to $15,000.

I remember sitting down with an industry friend around July 2016 over a glass of scotch, and he commented, "You guys are killing it, you're doing great." Then he asked, out of the blue, "But out of curiosity, are you happy?"

I only had to think for a split second before responding, "Honestly," I said, "On a scale of one to ten, I am at about a three on the happy scale."

I started asking myself some hard questions. "Am I making money for money's sake? Do I really have the freedom I've been chasing? What does success actually mean to me? Is having a work–life balance even possible?"

This is when I really began to adopt the RELAX method into my own working life. If my success wasn't on my terms, if my business owned me versus the other way around, it was having the opposite effect on my life from the goals that had inspired me to be an entrepreneur in the first place. Whenever it felt like my business was crushing my happiness and stealing my freedom, I needed to re-evaluate and adjust my ways.

Over a decade ago, I read a book called *The 4-Hour Workweek* by Tim Ferriss. That book changed my life. It helped me realize I have never believed in the "deferred-life plan" that most Americans are chasing. See if this sounds familiar: work your ass off for thirty-five to forty years then retire at age sixty, just as your body is deteriorating to the point where you can't do any of the things you love to do.

Tim proposes, "Why not take the usual twenty- to thirty-year retirement and redistribute it throughout life instead of saving it all for the end?"[36]

I hate to use my dad as an example, but months before retiring, he had to have a hip replaced, and he's waiting for his second hip to be replaced now. The things he really loves to

---

36   Timothy Ferriss, *The 4-Hour Workweek* (New York: Crown Publishers, 2007), 234.

do, like running and golfing, he's not able to do like he was in his thirties and forties.

In 2016, I was on this track. I was seeing my wife and daughter one hour a day max, pushing myself to the limit at work, chasing as much money as I could.

The year 2016 was the second in a row that I had not heeded Ferriss's advice to take an extended vacation since I started in business in 2008.

I had forgotten what was important to me, why I was working. To top it off, I had gained fifty pounds from eating out almost every meal and ignoring my health. As Tim Ferriss says, I was becoming "the fat man in the red BMW convertible."[37]

I was more worried about accumulating money than about the things that really get me excited about life, which are traveling with my family and spending time in the ocean.

Most high achievers stay on this track their entire careers, dreaming about the day they can retire and sip piña coladas on a beach somewhere. The problem is for most go-getters, this sedentary lifestyle, sitting on a beach under a palm tree, is only appealing for a couple weeks.

After two weeks or so, the high achiever does not feel fulfilled sitting on a beach. They cannot sit still long enough to enjoy themselves and will inevitably be looking for the next challenge to take on. I know, I've tried it.

After about the tenth day of sipping piña coladas, I'd be trying to figure out how to start my own beachfront bar. I'd be looking for land for sale, analyzing where I could source the rum directly from the manufacturer, and mapping out how to create a chain of beachfront piña colada bars.

---

37 Ferriss, *4-Hour Workweek*, 52–53.

On one of my two-month-long sabbaticals in Nicaragua, we were looking for a rental house and stumbled upon a commercial space for rent in San Juan del Sur, Nicaragua. It was in an amazing location, three blocks from the beach, right on the corner, across from the town's central park and church. It had tons of foot traffic all day from tourists and locals alike. The lightbulb went off, "This is an opportunity. We have to make something out of this." So, along with a friend, I decided to build a little twenty-five-person stadium-seating movie theater.

It was not an easy project because the space was previously an office. It took a couple months to convert the space: knock down a wall, close off all the light, install great air conditioning, and put in the sound and projector systems. We also had to build the platforms for the stadium seating and install leather chairs.

It was a fun project, and I was happy with the final product. The only problem was our market research wasn't done very effectively. Most tourists on vacation, it turned out, would rather spend $4 and two hours drinking at a beach bar than watching a movie. Most of our true clientele ended up being locals, paying the discounted local rate of $1 to see a show and reducing our profits to virtually nothing. Regardless, we hung on for a year and a half, earning about a tenth of what we had projected. It was a great learning experience.

A year prior to the movie theater venture was when I made the life-changing decision to take an extended trip to Central America to learn Spanish. While I've already touched on this time in Nicaragua, I'll briefly reiterate that it was arguably the best four months of my life. Every morning, five days a week, I took three hours of Spanish classes. I volunteered teaching kids English for an hour before lunch time. I surfed and read books in a hammock in the afternoons, and in the evenings, I enjoyed dancing and singing karaoke at the beach bars for pure immersion into the language.

The last two months, I stayed at a beachfront hostel with a private room for $7 a night with my girlfriend, who would later become my wife. Not $70, $7 a night. Two hundred and ten dollars a month. Literally on the beach, with great surfing waves fifty steps away.

What I couldn't learn in four years of Spanish in high school and two more years of independent study in my adult life I packed into four short months and came back to the States more fluent than ever. And I've already mentioned how invaluable my fluency in Spanish has been for my business success.

Something I've yet to discuss about my time in Nicaragua is how it changed my outlook on life. The people have nothing material-wise, often living on $100 to $300 per month with dirt floors in their houses, but they are rich in spirit. They are some of the happiest, most welcoming people you'll ever meet, with strong family ties and a great sense of humor. Homelessness and drug addiction appear to be almost non-existent relative to Southern California.

Going through life as fast as you can, staying on the work-to-buy-more treadmill, is clearly not creating more happiness. See the United States, with the highest depression, drug abuse, and suicide rates of any developed country in the world.

During your time off, aspire to learn how to slow down and appreciate living. Let the experiences affect you, change you, and make you grow. Learn how good we have it in the US and how most of our problems are "first-world problems" that the rest of the world's population would find to be trivial.

Are you stressed out and anxious because you can't pay your $3,000 mortgage or your $600-a-month car payment? Try living in a house with running water only six hours a day, daily electricity blackouts, and dirt floors for just a month. I promise it'll change your perspective.

I believe in the old adage, "Work hard, play hard," as a business owner in the United States. We actually have "Work hard, play hard" as one of our four company values.

When I am off work, it is very hard for me to detach, turn myself off, and relax unless I have geographically removed myself from the location of my business, preferably to a different time zone.

Enjoy the satisfaction you get from your work but only if you can maintain the balance to enjoy the things you love to do outside of work.

To this day, whenever I speak with a financial planner, the first question they ask is, "When are you planning to retire?" Followed by the inevitable second question, "How much do you need when you reach retirement age?" Or "What's your number?"

Most people in our culture have an arbitrary number of $1 million up to $100 million, which is what they "need" to retire. For even my most ambitious entrepreneur friends, that means indefinite working years leading to an ambiguous pot of gold at the end of the rainbow.

I recently had this conversation with a friend named Ben, who's raising venture capital for a software platform similar to Angi or the Better Business Bureau. I saw the value in the idea, and I started asking him questions.

"How much are you looking to sell it for once you have it built?"

"Fifty million dollars up to $100 million."

"What are you going to do with $50 million?"

"A lot of things—buy a yacht, charitable causes, scholarships, etc."

"You're fifty-two, how much longer do you plan on living? Twenty years?"

"Yeah, probably about that." (Ben is not the healthiest guy.)

"So you're telling me, if someone offered you $5 million, you wouldn't take it?"

"No, no way."

"You could live on, after paying taxes, around $3,000 dollars per week without working at all for the rest of your life, and you wouldn't take that?"

"No, no way."

Who knows if Ben will ever meet his own expectations and finally take some time off.

My encouragement to any budding entrepreneur would be to decide on a monthly amount as your retirement income. It doesn't matter if it's $5,000 per month or $5,000 per week. After some time in the grind, take off for one whole month and live on your self-prescribed monthly retirement income.

Give yourself the gift of an extended vacation for a month, trying as best you can to not work in your business while you're gone.

The tradition of sabbaticals from biblical times was to work for six years then take the seventh year off for rest and rejuvenation. So based on Leviticus's sage wisdom, if you've been in the grind for six years or longer, you owe yourself one year off. Or how about this? If one whole year off scares you, spread out two months per year for the next six years. Or three months a year for the next four years.

One month at a time is a great starting point. You will renew your goals and realize what you're working for, usually time with friends and family and maybe some travel. After about the third week of one of these mini-sabbaticals, you will start to settle in and actually feel rested and rejuvenated.

I would argue you should try to schedule one of these extended vacations one to three times a year, depending on your tolerance for leaving your business by itself.

This time off is required to continue grinding as an entrepreneur at an effective level without promoting burnout. It is also a great stress test to see how much your business depends on you as an information bottleneck or a sales or marketing rainmaker.

There are hundreds of books on the study of happiness. Since the end of the Industrial Revolution, the most prevailing piece of advice in all these books has been one thing: "Never ever retire." Retirement signifies the end, and the end of your working life usually means the end of you feeling you have purpose in this world, leaving you lost, without a productive pursuit to stay engaged.

Why not spread these sabbaticals out throughout your working life?

Why not taste some of the sweet nectar, the rewards of your hard work, while you're in your thirties, forties, and fifties instead of waiting until you're sixty years old?

Let me set something straight. I'm not saying you should be a total ball of stress during the months you are working and then finally chill out on your extended trips. The RELAX approach to business is designed to give you the mentality it takes to have enduring happiness and success on your own terms. For the amount of time we spend working, work should be fulfilling and enjoyable but not the end-all, be-all of your life. After all, "All work and no play makes Jack a dull boy."

What I am saying is Type A people, go-go-go obsessive compulsive types, i.e., most of us crazy entrepreneurs, need a break now and then. And they need to be scheduled or else you'll never really allow yourself to take your foot off the gas. Think of what you really loved doing at age twelve or thirteen, before money was in the picture. Now, go do some of those things again on your time off. Go be a kid again. You'll be amazed at how you feel when you get back to the office.

CHAPTER 11—ACTION STEPS

- Decide if burnout has ever been an issue for you while pushing toward your entrepreneurial goals. If it has, make some changes.
- Ask yourself, "What if retirement wasn't an option? What would that look like?"
- The average retirement age is sixty-four, and the average life expectancy is seventy-seven. That gives you thirteen years, or 156 months, of retirement. Now, take seventy-seven minus your age. Let's say you are thirty years old. One hundred fifty-six months of retirement divided by forty-seven years is 3.32 months or fourteen weeks. As such, fourteen weeks off per year should be your goal.
- Schedule regular planned time off every year. Start with a month at a time then try to work up to three or four months off a year and see how you feel. The results are astounding for motivation and energy.
- Practice doing the things you love to do, that you wish to pursue in your retirement. Is it more time for exercise? Sports you used to play but no longer have time for? Reading more or writing a book?

WHAT IT'S ALL ABOUT

"It isn't what you have or who you are or where you are or what you are doing that makes you happy or unhappy. It is what you think about it."

—Dale Carnegie

I was fortunate enough to take a month off in Hawaii this past winter with my family. We enjoyed the near-perfect weather, hiking, and going to the beach as our friends in California endured a freak snowstorm and record low temperatures. Sometimes, I have to pinch myself as a reminder that a month off in Hawaii isn't possible when you're working for somebody else.

I was able to bring my kids out in the ocean to surf with me several times a week, taking full advantage of the warm ocean water. My son Jacob, who's now seven, has gone tandem surfing with me for the last couple years. Paddling out one day with Jacob on the front of our soft-top surfboard, he blurted out, "I want to surf by myself!" To be completely honest, I didn't think he was going to have the courage to surf on his own for a year or two more. But just like that, he was ready.

I got him turned around and in position and pushed him onto the very next wave not two minutes after he made his brave declaration. He stood up and rode the wave almost all the way to the beach, knees bent and arms spread out wide, eyes focused on the beach, just like we'd practiced a hundred times before. I let out a screeching yelp—*YEE-HAW*!—and swam over to him to give him a high five and a big hug. He beamed with pure joy, grinning from ear to ear. My eyes welled up as I couldn't contain the raw emotion of a proud father watching my independent little surfer.

He followed up his first wave by catching eight more, one after another, more confident each and every time, assuming his warrior stance and gliding along the top of the water. Afterwards, we called Grandma and Grandpa to brag and celebrated with triple scoops of Häagen-Dazs ice cream, reveling in the glory of the day and telling stories about it into the night.

I remember thinking, *This is what it's all about.*

This is why we work: to experience moments of pure joy and excitement, like helping my seven-year-old son stand up on his first waves. All the times we must get uncomfortable or discipline ourselves to be a little better culminate in being able to be present for these peak moments in our loved ones' lives.

Sometimes, we get caught up in the how-tos and grimy brass-tack details of how to become a successful business person. But it all boils down to this: harness your enthusiasm and go have fun doing something you love to do. And if your work isn't something you love to do, for God's sake, make sure your time off is exciting and filled with special moments with your friends and family.

The life of an entrepreneur, if nothing else, should be an exciting adventure. One of unparalleled challenge and an incredible amount of freedom.

Hopefully, this book has provided some tools and inspiration to help you wherever you are on your journey. Like you, I'm a student on a path, learning all the time. Understand that we're all just trying to figure it out. You will make mistakes along the way, as we all do. Don't be discouraged, don't give up, just take one day at a time.

I wish you the best of luck on your adventure.

MICHAEL WEBER AFFIRMATIONS OCTOBER 21, 2021

Michael Weber, meet Michael Weber, a man designed for success. Ever since he was a little boy, he has excelled in everything he has done. Straight As in school, honors student in college, leader in running, setting records everywhere he ran. He will continue to excel. He will think only of success, only of progress and prosperity.

He, Michael Weber, has the courage to succeed. Fear should never get in his way. He has faced his fears and achieved everything he has sought to achieve over the last fifteen years. He was a leading alarm and insurance salesman, knocking on doors in cities all over the country for three years. He led successful sales offices in Denver, Colorado, San Jose, California, and Houston. He wanted to learn Spanish, so he left his business in Houston, moved to Nicaragua for four months in 2012, and learned fluent Spanish. As a bonus, he met his beautiful wife, Zeneyda, and he has a great, harmonious marriage and four amazing, beautiful kids. A smart, beautiful thirteen-year-old daughter Nicol; a happy, bilingual, adventurous seven-year-old boy Jacob; a handsome, healthy five-year-old boy Jeremiah; and a precious new baby, Christopher.

In 2013 and 2014, he aggressively saved and invested more than half of his earnings while being the best salesman in the company, selling $1 million of roofing for two consecutive years. He built a movie theater called Cine en Paradise out of raw office space in San Juan del Sur, Nicaragua. Although it wasn't a success, he learned about doing business internationally, how to build something from nothing, and how to coordinate workers in Spanish.

He wanted to learn how to sell solar, so he moved to California to learn the solar business at the beginning of 2015. In his first year of business, his company sold $1.8 million of solar panels, and in his second year, it doubled that number to $3.6 million. In 2018, his company sold nearly $6 million of solar. At the beginning of 2019, Michael started a roofing business using a $350,000 connection he made with his business partner in Nicaragua, Bob, and his friend's brother's contractor's license to get the company off the ground. Within the first four years of launching the roofing business, he and his business partner were able to sell $17 million of roofs.

Fear will never get in Michael Weber's way. He has been skydiving twice; he has swum in thirty-foot waves; he has surfed fifteen-foot waves. He has held his breath diving through lava tubes thirty feet below the ocean. He has completed an Olympic distance triathlon and six 26.2-mile marathons. In 2021, he ran the hardest trail course he's ever run. It was in Steamboat Springs, Colorado. In 2018, he completed a fifty-mile running race, one of the toughest in the country, in the mountains of the Cleveland National Forest in Southern California in under thirteen hours. In 2020, he ran a marathon on Maui and broke through the four-hour barrier for the first time.

Michael Weber THINKS BIG in everything he does. He appreciates that he lives in the most prosperous time period in the history of the world, in the richest country with the highest standard of living humans have ever known. He lives in the United States of America, in truly the Golden Age of Civilization that humans have looked forward to for thousands of years, where people living on welfare live like the kings and queens of the past. He understands that taking big risks means big rewards and to be temporarily broke is much better than being poor or enslaved to a weekly paycheck. He knows that saving and investing 30 percent to 40 percent of his income is one of the most important factors that has made him successful, and he will continue to set savings goals to take advantage of opportunities as they come to him.

Michael does not let petty things get in his way or annoy him. He realizes the best way to his success is to help others find success and give out praise and compliments whenever possible. He knows that feeling good through proper eating and exercise, along with planned personal development through reading, audiobooks in the car, and listening to motivational speakers every morning, is the best way to keep his mental attitude on track. He recognizes that going to Toastmasters and comedy clubs and welcoming any public-speaking engagements are all part of the formula for success. He will continue to study the lives of successful people who have gone before him and be grateful for everything he has.

On November 1, 2016, he embarked on an exciting and challenging chapter of his life—to Nicaragua to build his hotel, Pacific Vista, on the beach and sell off some of his property on the hill overlooking the Pacific Ocean. Between November 2016 and February 2017, he raised $175,000 dollars from four different investors, with 1.5 acres of land backings for their investments. He still maintains 75 percent ownership in the project on the beach and 10.75 acres of land on the hill to work with in the future.

Starting in July 2017, he returned to California to continue pursuing his success with his solar business, riding this giant wave of momentum that the solar industry has in California, building an office in San Bernardino County. He has built an awesome sales team and will continue building. His solar and roofing company will sell a total of $18 million dollars by the end of 2023. It will not be easy, but nothing worth having ever comes easy. He will work with his partner Bob to build $6.4 million of condominiums on his beachfront property in Nicaragua. Despite juggling several projects, Michael will keep a good balance between work, family, and play time.

Within two years, in 2025, Michael will be able to spend six months a year traveling with his family. He will become the waterman that he was fifteen years ago and spend hours a day alongside his kids in the ocean—surfing, diving, and spearfishing. His kids, Nicol, Jacob, Jeremiah, and Christopher, and his wife, Zeneyda, will learn the beauty of growing up as a family on the beach and with nature instead of in front of the television, like most Americans.

He will have amazing success buying and selling land and building condominiums in Nicaragua and all over Central America. He will create an adventure volunteer tourism company to broaden the minds of high school and college kids and show them how good they have it in the US. He will bring his family together for long vacations in Hawaii starting in the summer of 2026.

He will use his drive, enthusiasm, and thought mastery to run his business and his family life in a beautiful, balanced way, always looking for the next adventure. NOW GO TO IT, MICHAEL!

TEMPLATE TO CREATE YOUR OWN AFFIRMATIONS

[Your name], meet [Your name], a man/woman designed for success. Ever since s/he was a little boy/girl, s/he has excelled in everything s/he has done. [Accomplishment] in school. Leader in [something you excelled at during childhood or teenage years.] S/he will continue to excel. S/he will think only of success, only of progress and prosperity.

S/he, [Your name], has the courage to succeed. Fear should never get in his/her way. S/he has faced his/her fears and achieved everything s/he has sought to achieve over the last [number of working] years. S/he was a leading [your profession or career choice]. S/he wanted to learn [something you successfully learned], so s/he [strong move to achieve or learn something] and learned [that thing you put your mind to].

S/he met his/her beautiful [your spouse's name], and s/he has a great, harmonious marriage and [number of kids] amazing, beautiful kids. [Insert your kids names and some positive adjectives for them, if you have kids.]

[Talk about one failure you had and what it taught you in a positive light.]

[Follow it up with three to four successes that you describe in detail.]

Fear will never get in [your name]'s way.

[Specify three to four things you've done where you conquered your own fear and took action anyway.]

[Your name] THINKS BIG in everything s/he does. S/he appreciates that s/he lives in the most prosperous time period in the history of the world, with the highest standard of living humans have ever known. S/he lives in [your country], in truly the Golden Age of Civilization that humans have looked forward to for thousands of years, where people living on welfare live like the kings and queens of the past.

S/he understands that taking big risks means big rewards and to be temporarily broke is much better than being poor or enslaved to a weekly paycheck. S/he knows that saving and investing 30 to 40 percent of his/her income is the most important factor that has made him/her successful and s/he will continue to set savings goals to take advantage of opportunities as they come to him/her.

[Your name] does not let petty things get in his/her way or annoy him/her. S/he realizes the best way to his/her success is to help others find success and give out praise and compliments whenever possible. S/he knows that feeling good through proper eating and exercise, along with planned personal development with reading, audiobooks in the car, and listening to motivational speakers every morning, is the best way to keep his/her mental attitude on track. S/he recognizes that going to Toastmasters and comedy clubs and welcoming any public-speaking engagements are all part of the formula for success. S/he will continue to study the lives of successful people who have gone before him/her and be grateful for everything s/he has.

[Write in one or two paragraphs of career or life accomplishments that you're proud of, in detail, consecutively]

Next year, [your name] will be able to [major goal you're working toward.] Starting in two years, [your name] will be able to [another major goal you're working toward].

His/her kids, [kids' names] and his/her spouse [spouse's name] will learn [whatever values you want to instill in them when you're able to be with them more full time.]

S/he will have amazing success [doing whatever you will do when you're partially or fully retired, including one thing to give back your time or money].

S/he will bring his/her extended family [wherever you want to bring your family that's always been a dream location for you.]

S/he will use his/her drive, enthusiasm, and thought mastery to run his/her business and his/her family life in a beautiful, balanced way, always looking for the next adventure. NOW GO TO IT, [Your name]!

ACKNOWLEDGMENTS

Thank you, Mom and Dad. All I've ever wanted is to make you proud.

Thank you, Mom, for teaching me my love of reading and how to make friends wherever I go. You gave me my gift of gab and my ability to laugh at life and not take things too seriously.

Thank you, Dad, for teaching me the values of hard work, discipline, and loyalty by your example and encouraging me to finish what I start. You are the most solid, consistent person I've ever met.

Thank you to my brothers for always keeping me humble. Thanks to Matt Weber for inspiring me to write and being my sounding board all the way. Thanks to Timmy Weber for always calling my bullshit and reminding me I'm still an idiot. Thanks to David Weber for being the brains of the family and for being the first person to read my first draft and give me eighteen pages of feedback.

Thanks to Teddy Argus for always being a good friend and taking the time out of your busy life to talk about my book and to give me advice and ideas.

Thanks to my editors, Nancy Pile and Mark Chait, for being extremely encouraging and complimentary while tearing apart my book and making me do the work to ensure it flows and reads well.

Thank you to Dave Pond, John Speed and my business partner David Mitchell, for teaching me the ways of the Slow Burn Entrepreneur, and providing inspiration for this book.

ABOUT THE AUTHOR

MICHAEL WEBER is a serial entrepreneur and founder of Summit Solar & Roofing and Summit Marketing in the United States, as well as the owner and founder of Pacific Vista Enterprises in Nicaragua. His companies have grossed upwards of $25 million. His hobbies include trail running, surfing, diving, and spearfishing. He currently resides in Southern California with his wife and four kids and spends as much time as possible on the beaches of Nicaragua and Hawaii with his family. He is a first-time author.

www.ingramcontent.com/pod-product-compliance
Lightning Source LLC
Chambersburg PA
CBHW030512210326
41597CB00013B/886